The Old Testament
through story and symbol

Jan Thompson

Edward Arnold
A division of Hodder & Stoughton

LONDON   MELBOURNE   AUCKLAND

First published in Great Britain 1985
Second impression 1988

British Library Cataloguing in Publication Data
Thompson, Jan
  The Old Testament through story and
    symbol
  1. Bible. O.T.—Text-books
  I. Title
  221   BS11402

ISBN 0-7131-7319-X

For my God children,
Katherine Francis
and Graeme James

Illustrated by Robina Green

Acknowledgements

The Publishers would like to thank the following
for permission to include copyright material:
Oxford and Cambridge University Presses for
material from the New English Bible © 1970,
used by permission, and Oxford University Press
for the illustration from S.H. Hooke, *In the
Beginning*, p.13.

The Publishers wish to thank the following for
their permission to reproduce copyright
illustrations:

Syndication International: p 10 l; Roy
Peters/LINK: p 10 r; Monica Kendall: p 11;
British Museum: pp 12, 20, 21, 25; Tate Gallery:
pp 14, 77, 78 l & r, 85; Mansell Collection: pp 19,
26, 30, 35, 39, 43, 47, 64, 71, 80, 89, 91; Scottish
Tourist Board: p 22; Juliette Soester: p 27; David
Richardson: p 37; A Vanderstock: p 40;
M R Thompson: p 41; A F Kersting: p 49;
Documentation photographique de la Reunion des
musees nationaux/Le Louvre: pp 52 l & r, 54;
Topham Picture Library: p 53; C V Middleton &
Son (photographers): p 55; Jan Thompson: pp 57,
76, 87; Ronald Sheridan's Photo Library: p 65;
Popperfoto: pp 66, 82; Christian Aid (Sophie
Baker): p 73; British Library: p 83; NASA: p 93.

Printed and bound in Great Britain for Edward
Arnold, the educational, academic and medical
publishing division of Hodder and Stoughton
Limited, Mill Road, Dunton Green, Sevenoaks,
Kent, by J. W. Arrowsmith Ltd, Bristol

Contents

Preface

This is a course on the Old Testament, written for lower to middle secondary school pupils. It covers the most famous stories but explains them in the light of modern scholarship and with a particular eye to symbolism. The different types of literature in the Old Testament are presented, both to emphasise its diversity and to help pupils see the different ways in which beliefs can be expressed.

The Old Testament can still hold an important place in the R.E. syllabus. It is essential to know something about it in order to understand Judaism and Christianity, and in order to appreciate Western culture: its laws, literature, art and music. Also, in studying a sacred book, we deal with one important aspect of religion. Finally, like all great literature, the Old Testament is full of human interest. It explores questions which are of fundamental importance to mankind and offers answers which can be discussed in the light of our own age. Much of it is presented in story form, which has the power to stir up our emotions and get us interested and involved.

This book emphasises the symbolic nature of the Old Testament, and of religious language in general. This is not to deny the historical basis of the Old Testament, and yet it is not seen simply as history. The truth of the Bible goes deeper than this, since it deals with religious feelings and beliefs which can often *only* be expressed symbolically. I have therefore drawn attention to particular symbols and also to the symbolic nature of many of the different types of story in the Old Testament.

There is a wide selection of assignments and it is up to the teacher to choose the ones that are most suitable and to give help with these. Not all of the questions require written answers; sometimes discussion is more useful. The assignments often draw out further ideas from the text and show their relevance to life today. They also encourage some first-hand reading of the Bible.

A set of blackline masters is available to accompany this text book. It provides worksheets and information sheets for the pupils to have. Their purpose is (a) to give more practice in grasping some of the ideas presented in the book; (b) to develop some of the themes or draw out their modern relevance; (c) to give more information and assignments, including revision exercises; (d) to provide pupils with some maps and charts from the book; and (e) to quote biblical passages so that some assignments can be done, perhaps for homework, without needing Bibles.

J.T.

1 Introduction

The Old Testament

The Old Testament is the first and longest part of the Christian Bible. Yet it was not written by Christians, for it already existed as the Jewish Holy Scriptures. The first Christians were Jews (as was Jesus Christ) and they used their existing scriptures to help them understand God's plan in sending the Christ. They saw the promises God made to his chosen people in the Old Testament come true in Jesus and in the Church, both of which are written about in the New Testament. So the Old Testament is an important part of the Christian Bible for it is seen as Part 1 of a story which reaches a happy ending in Part 2, the New Testament.

Books in the Old Testament

The word **Bible** comes from the Greek for 'book' or 'books'. Although the Holy Bible is usually printed within one cover, there are many different books inside it.

The first section of the Bible is the Pentateuch, which simply means 'Five Books'. This is the oldest part of the Bible, completed nearly 2,500 years ago. It includes stories about the beginning of the world, the earliest human beings and the ancestors of the Jews. It also contains many Jewish laws.

Most of the other Old Testament books may be regarded as prophetic because they are concerned in some way with God's spokesmen, the prophets. The books of Joshua, Judges, Samuel and Kings tell stories about the early prophets. Other books, named after each prophet, record the words of the great prophets of the eighth to the fifth centuries BC, since their words were considered to be inspired by God. There are three very long such books, named after Isaiah, Jeremiah and Ezekiel. They are called the Major Prophets. There are also twelve Minor Prophets which are very short books, some of only two or three chapters.

The rest of the Old Testament is a mixture of material. Some of it is very ancient, like some of the poems in the book of Psalms and some of the wise sayings in the book of Proverbs, which are about 3,000 years old. At

the other extreme is the book of Daniel, the youngest book in the Old Testament, which probably dates from the second century BC. It contains mysterious visions of the end of the world.

We cannot say with certainty when all these books of the Old Testament were written nor when they were accepted as Holy Scripture. The making of the Jewish scriptures was a long and complicated process which was only finished towards the end of the first century AD. Some of the earliest material had been composed over 1,000 years before this and had been passed down for centuries by word of mouth before being put in writing. The words of the prophets may well have been written down soon after their time but the final editing of the prophetic books probably did not take place before the fourth century BC. Most of the books of the Old Testament were put together from material which had come down from different ages and which reflected different religious views. The Old Testament writers had to weave together these different strands and they did not always manage to hide the loose ends. In our study of the Old Testament we shall sometimes note earlier or later material in the stories and also the religious ideas of the final writers themselves.

So the Old Testament is a selection of different types of religious books, written over a period of 1,000 years, by many different people. What these books have in common is that, in some way, they all tell the story of God's dealings with his chosen people, the Jews, and of how this people grew in their understanding of God. All the books gradually became accepted by the Jews as having God's authority behind them and so they were collected together and regarded as the Word of God.

Assignments

1 Look at the list of Old Testament books at the front of the Bible and count how many there are. (There will be more if you are using a Catholic Bible. Your teacher may wish to explain what the Apocrypha is.)
2 List the books of the Pentateuch.
3 Find the list of the Twelve Minor Prophets, beginning with Hosea.
4 Which prophetic book comes at the very end of the Old Testament?
5 Learn to spell the name Isaiah correctly.

Old Testament history

It is not possible to understand the Old Testament without having some idea of the history which lies behind it. The *Old Testament History Chart* on p. 7 outlines the most important periods.

No one knows exactly when the Patriarchs lived, but they must be placed somewhere far back in the second millennium BC. They are the forefathers of the Jews who lived in and around Canaan (later called the Promised Land, the Land of Israel, Judaea, Palestine and the Holy Land). At the end of this period, the families of the Patriarchs, known as Hebrews at this early stage, were living in Egypt. They had been driven there by drought in Canaan and they were eventually enslaved by the Egyptians.

Nor do we know the date of the Exodus, even though it is probably the most important event in the Old Testament. The Exodus is seen as the moment in history when God adopted this persecuted, immigrant population as his chosen people. He appointed Moses to organise their escape from Egypt and to lead them through the wilderness to the Promised Land. Some scholars believe that this took place as early as 1440 BC, whereas many others place it around 1250 BC.

After this Wilderness Period came the periods of Conquest and Settlement in Canaan, at first under Joshua and then under a number of leaders called Judges. During this time the Hebrews lived in their separate family tribes.

By the end of the eleventh century BC, it became necessary to unite these various tribes under one ruler if they were to withstand the force of surrounding enemies. So a monarchy was established. At first the northern and southern tribes worked together, but after about one hundred years their underlying divisions led to a breakaway kingdom being set up in the north, known as Israel. The southern kingdom was called Judah and had Jerusalem as its capital city. The separate northern kingdom survived for two hundred years before being destroyed by foreign enemies to the north. The southern kingdom lasted almost one hundred and fifty years longer but eventually Jerusalem was conquered and its inhabitants were taken into exile in Babylon.

The destruction of the monarchy came as a severe blow to God's chosen people and the Exile gave them time to come to terms with it. Their religious faith survived, and eventually they were allowed to return to their land and rebuild their lives there. This is known as the Restoration. After this, apart from one hundred years of independence following the Maccabean Wars, the Jews of Old Testament times remained under foreign overlords: after the Babylonians came the Persians, then the Greeks, and finally the Romans.

Assignments

6 Read carefully through the *Old Testament History Chart* and make sure you know what everything refers to.

Old Testament History Chart

BC

	The Patriarchs
1800 (?)	ABRAHAM reached Canaan
	ISAAC
	JACOB
	12 SONS e.g. JOSEPH in Egypt
1250 (?)	*Exodus*
	under MOSES out of Egypt
	Wilderness Period under MOSES
	Conquest
	under JOSHUA, of Canaan
	Settlement under JUDGES
c1020	*Monarchy*
	united kingdom under SAUL
	DAVID
	SOLOMON
922	2 kingdoms:
	ISRAEL (N); JUDAH (S)
	prophets: ELIJAH
	AMOS
	HOSEA
	ISAIAH
722	Fall of Israel
	JEREMIAH
586	Fall of Judah
	EZEKIEL
	Exile in Babylon
539	*Return and Restoration*
450 (?)	NEHEMIAH and EZRA in Jerusalem
336	*Greek Period*
167	Maccabean Wars

7 Learn the following list of important
 periods in Old Testament history:
    Period of the Patriarchs
    Exodus and Wilderness Period
    Conquest and Settlement
    Monarchy
    Exile and Restoration
8 Write a sentence on each of the periods
 in No. 7 explaining their meaning.

Symbolism in the Old Testament

It may seem, from what you have learned
so far, that the Old Testament is concerned
only with history; but it is more than that.
The Old Testament has many different types
of stories. Some are mainly historical, with
details that can be checked against other
records and archaeological remains. But most
are in some way symbolic — their importance
lies not in history but in the religious truths
to which they point, truths that go beyond
simple facts.

We cannot just say that the historical
stories are true and the symbolic ones are
not, for the question of truth is more than
simply one of 'Did it actually happen?' This
means that we should not take the stories at
their face value. To do them justice, we must
ask what they stand for, and what religious
truth they are trying to express.

Many different kinds of stories have this
extra, religious or symbolic meaning. Some
are familiar to us today, like **proverbs** and
poetry. There are **parables**, stories with a
special meaning, like the ones Jesus used and
which are recorded in the New Testament.
From television, you may have come across
the terms **saga** (those long stories of family
intrigue) and **epic**. There are **legends** — stories
that have grown up around a historical
character to illustrate what sort of person he
or she was. There are also **myths**, elaborate
stories to express how the world came to be

as it is, expressing truths that are beyond
scientific or historical evidence.

All of these forms of symbolic language
will be found in the Old Testament. Each in
its own way is trying to express *more than*
simple historical fact. These stories combine
to make the Old Testament of religious
importance to people today and not simply a
record of the past.

Signs and symbols

As well as symbolic stories, there are many
other symbols in the Old Testament. For
instance, names, objects like a garden or a
rainbow, and actions like taking off shoes or
dressing up as a slave, all take on special
meaning.

We still make use of symbols today, so let
us think about what they are, and how and
why they are used.

A person who waves to you is not just
exercising his arm, he is expressing friendship.
If you put up your hand in class, it generally
means that you want to ask a question; but if
you do the same thing at an auction, you'll
end up bidding for something. In each case, a
simple action communicates a special meaning.
It has become a sign.

Signs and symbols are an important part of our everyday lives. If you wear a school uniform it is a sign that you belong to a particular school, and the colour of a badge may indicate your school house or team. On the way to school you may catch a bus with a number on the front as a sign of where it is going. The driver will stop at a bus stop and obey traffic signs. If you hear the school bell ringing when you arrive, it may be that you are only just in time.

Numbers, colours, pictures, sounds and actions can all take on a deeper, symbolic meaning. They can stand for something else. Sometimes these signs are chosen for no apparent reason, like the coloured stripes on a tie. Others have an obvious connection with their meaning, like the pictures of children or cattle on the traffic signs that warn that they may be crossing the road. Signs are useful abbreviations. Without them we should not be able to give quick, clear messages to people like the bus driver.

Assignments

9 Try to find ten signs that you pass on your way to and from school.
10 Think of all the ways in which the letter 'x' is used symbolically, to stand for something else.
11 Draw and explain the meaning of two signs which are commonly accepted but which would be meaningless until they were explained.
12 Draw and explain the meaning of at least two signs which do convey their meaning in themselves.

Some signs are important and yet we can remain detached from them. It would not really matter to us what road signs were used as long as all motorists recognised them. Others, however, can stir up deep emotions in us so that we become personally involved in them and do not like them to be changed. These are often called symbols. A football scarf can represent your feelings of loyalty to a particular team, or a flag may show your patriotism. Such symbols can strengthen and encourage the feelings that they express. Why else should supporters of the opposing team hurl abuse at a simple scarf trailing from a car window; or a soldier weep with joy to see his flag hoisted at the end of a battle?

Some symbols are very ancient and crop up all over the world, like light and darkness to represent good and evil, or fire to represent God's presence. It seems that people used and responded to these symbols naturally, without needing to have them explained.

Symbols help us to express what is difficult to put into ordinary words. Most of us, for instance, would find it very difficult to describe the love we feel for someone. It is not like describing something that can be seen. Love is abstract: it has no size, weight, colour or shape. Love cannot be described like a scientific fact, but it can be described in poetry, or symbolised in a kiss or a Valentine card.

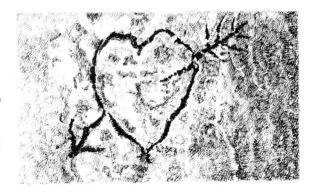

13 Describe, draw or write out one symbol that you feel personally involved in (like the school song), and explain the meaning it has for you.
14 Give two examples of things, other than love, which are abstract.

Religious symbols

Symbolism is especially important in religion. People may experience deep feelings like that of unworthiness, of being sorry for their sins, of being forgiven and accepted, of being at peace with themselves, of being at one with other members of their religion, or being filled with joy and of overflowing with praise. Such abstract emotions can be expressed best through words and actions that symbolise them.

Such symbols usually have some obvious connection with what they represent e.g. outward washing can represent inner purity. The worshipper expresses his or her feelings through these symbolic actions, or by using symbolic words.

Hindus regard their rivers in India as holy. Here you can see some Hindus performing religious acts of washing in the river. This symbolises the washing away of their sins. Notice the Hindu holy-man among them, with the long hair.

Religion is not just about feelings, but also about thoughts. A clear example of an abstract religious idea is belief in God. Religious people believe in God without asking that his existence should be proved scientifically. God is said to be supernatural, which means that God is greater than and different from things of this natural world. So to say that God exists does not mean that God lives in the same way as you or I do. We use human images for God because man is the highest and most personal form of creation that we know, and because we naturally think in these images.

For example, the Old Testament speaks of God's ears, eyes, mouth, hand and arm, but these are not to be taken literally. They are symbols which stand for something greater than themselves. We know that God does not hear, see, speak and act in the same way as we do, but it is difficult to express the ideas behind all this in any other way. Although there is no other way of speaking about God, we must remember when people say something like 'Our Father who art in heaven', that 'he' is of no sex, is fatherlike only in some ways, and cannot be found in any one particular place. The symbols we use are like arrows pointing us in the right direction, but they must not be taken literally or mistaken for the thing they point towards.

The Old Testament is full of symbolism and it cannot be understood properly without recognising this. We shall be seeing the importance of particular symbols and, as we study some of the most important stories of the Old Testament, we shall be paying special attention to the way in which they too may become symbols, pointing beyond themselves to abstract religious truths.

Assignments

15 Draw a number of faces, or pin-men, to express some of the religious feelings mentioned at the beginning of this section on religious symbols.

16 Look up the following passages and find out what symbols for God are used in them: Psalm 23 v. 1; Psalm 31 v. 2; Psalm 33 v. 20; Isaiah 6 v. 5; Isaiah 60 v. 19.

This is a silver coin struck in Judaea around 350 BC, under Persian rule. It shows God sitting on a winged wheel which perhaps symbolises the sun, and therefore light. The Jews were forbidden to make images of God, so the coin may have been struck by the Persian authorities.

2 In the beginning

The creation stories

The first book of the Old Testament is called **Genesis** which means 'origins', because it explores the beginnings of the world and of the Jewish people in particular. It starts with the words: 'In the beginning God created heaven and earth.' This is the opening of a creation story which probably dates from about 500 BC. It is set out in seven neat sections, corresponding to the seven days of the week, beginning with the appearance of light on the first day, and finishing with the arrival of men and women on the sixth. We are told that God rested from his creative work on the seventh day, just as the Jews keep this day of each week as the Sabbath, the holy day of rest.

Assignments

1 Read this story out loud in class, with seven different readers for each of the seven sections, and the whole class joining in the refrain: 'Evening came, and morning came, a . . . day.' The story is in Genesis ch. 1 v. 1—ch. 2 v. 4.
2 Draw a picture-strip with six squares to illustrate the six days of creation.

The book of Genesis continues with another creation story from an earlier period (about 850 BC). This is the story of Adam and Eve. It starts with the earth as a wasteland, instead of the waters of the first version. There is no reference to the time it took to create things, and this is its order of creation:

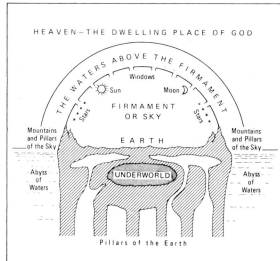

There are various references in the Old Testament which have led scholars to construct pictures like this one of the Hebrew idea of the universe. We cannot be sure that this shows exactly what the Hebrews believed: some of their descriptions differ, and ideas must have changed as time went on; also, some may be symbolic and not meant to be taken literally. We can be sure, however, that the Hebrews thought of the universe very differently from us today, and pictures like this one can help us to make sense of the creation story in Genesis chapter 1.

This imaginative picture shows God creating Adam. It was painted by William Blake in 1795. Why do you think he has painted the snake coiling around Adam?

i) man (ch. 2 v. 7)
ii) the garden in Eden (v. 8)
iii) trees of every kind (v. 9)
iv) animals and birds (v. 19)
v) woman (vv. 21—2)

Assignments

3 Make a note of the differences between the two creation stories in Genesis chapters 1 and 2.
4 Genesis ch. 2 v. 19 says that man was given the right to name all the animals. This act of naming is symbolic: it shows that man has power over the animal world.

a) Do you think we *do* have this power? Give reasons for your answer.
b) What responsibilities would such a power bring with it?
5 Discuss what Genesis ch. 2 vv. 20—5 tells us about the relationship between men and women.

Myths

You may have been surprised to discover that there are *two* quite distinct creation stories in the Bible. They are different from each other in style and details and come from periods hundreds of years apart. In our modern world we expect an account of creation to be scientific, and it is difficult for us to see how you can accept two sets of contradictory facts. Surely one of these stories must be right and the other one wrong! But the writer of Genesis did not think like that. He came from a people who were used to expressing their ideas and beliefs in stories called myths.

It is a pity that the word 'myth' is commonly used today to refer to something that is not true. (The word 'story' has been misused in a similar way, so that if your mother says to you 'Don't tell stories' she really means 'Don't tell lies.') The correct meaning of *a myth is a story full of symbolism* which digs deeper than scientific or historic facts *to express basic truth about life* which is difficult to express in any other way. Such stories answer the deep religious questions that we all ask at one time or another:
  i)   Why is there a world at all?
  ii) Why is the world as it is, with good things as well as terrible suffering?
  iii) Why are people here?
  iv) What responsibility do we have in the world?
  v)   What is the purpose of *my* life?
  Myths express the common view of life held by a whole people, rather than that of an individual author. They are told by one generation to the next in order to pass on the insights and values of that people. The first creation story in Genesis, with its orderly divisions and repeated refrains, looks as if it were composed to be recited by the people (as Christians repeat the Lord's Prayer and so come to know it and be influenced by its ideas).

Myths are stories in which a people express their deepest beliefs about life. So the creation stories would be more concerned with *why* the world was made than with *how* it was made. The editor of the Pentateuch found gems of truth in both creation stories and he would have seen no problem in including the old story of Adam and Eve alongside his more up-to-date version. After all, despite their differences, they both express the same basic beliefs that God is behind all that exists, that he created an orderly world and intended it to be a good place in which to live.

Assignments

6 Copy out the definition of myth which is printed in italics above.
7 Choose one of the questions (i)—(v) and give your own answer to it.
8 Can you think of any other important questions people ask about life which cannot simply be answered with scientific facts?

The Fall of Man

The second creation story in Genesis (the earliest version) continues into the story of the Fall of Man. It is the well-known story of how Adam and Eve give in to temptation and are punished for their sin by being driven from the Garden of Eden.

This story tackles the question of what went wrong with the world. If God meant the world to be good, why are we now in such a mess? Many people find that the answers it gives are as true today as they were when this myth started, nearly 3,000 years ago. I do not mean that you can ignore what your science teachers tell you about evolution, and that you can blame all the suffering in the world on two individuals called Adam and Eve. This story is not really about two individual characters, but about Everyman and Everywoman. Adam is a word which simply means 'man', (as the more modern English translations of the Bible recognise). Eve means 'life' in Hebrew, which is a fitting name for woman whose special role is as mother, the giver of life. This myth has deep insight into human nature which may still ring true for us today, since people do not seem to have changed very much down the ages. So it tells us about ourselves and about our relationship with God and the world.

The story is a tragedy: it begins in hope and ends in disaster. Man and woman are given the opportunity of living a heavenly existence in a wonderful garden where all their needs are provided for; but they are not satisfied. The woman is tempted by the snake to eat the fruit of a forbidden tree. She wants the one thing she cannot have. She is not satisfied with being human, but wants to know everything, like God. Once she has fallen to temptation, she pulls man down with her. They know they have sinned and are ashamed of themselves. (The need to cover their nakedness represents their loss of child-like innocence.) When the man is called to account by God for what he has done, he tries to excuse himself by blaming the woman, and she in turn blames the snake. They are driven from the garden as punishment and from now on their life must be a hard struggle and misery.

The main message of this story is that people have spoilt the world that God intended to be so good for them, through their own selfish greed. This selfish greed has been called by Christians 'original sin' because it seems to be in all human beings and continues to be their downfall.

Then the eyes of both of them were opened and they discovered that they were naked; so they stitched fig-leaves together and made themselves loincloths. (Genesis ch. 3 v. 7)

Assignments

9 Your teacher may wish you to read the story of the Fall of Man in Genesis ch. 3.
10 Using Genesis ch. 3 vv. 14—19, describe what life was like for the people who first told this myth. It helped them to understand why life was like this.
11 Make up a story of your own to show how selfish greed can ruin people's lives, their relationships or the world in which they live.
12 What is the opposite of selfish greed?
13 Read again the paragraph beginning 'The story is a tragedy . . .'. Is there anything there which you could say is fairly typical of human behaviour, and therefore still rings true today?
14 In this story, the snake is a symbol of evil. What other characters can you think of which sometimes represent evil? Illustrate this answer, if you want.

Noah's Ark

Most children in Western countries have come across the story of Noah's Ark. Even if you have never read the story, you may well have sung songs about it when you were younger or played with toy models of the ark and the animals. There is an obvious appeal in the story for children, since all the animals you can think of can be brought into the ark. But the story is really about judgement. Its message is that people's rejection of God brings about their destruction.

Briefly, the story tells how God despairs of the world he has created and he decides to sweep everything away in a great flood, and start again. The only good person is Noah, who is warned of the coming disaster and of how to escape. Following God's instructions, Noah builds a huge boat (Noah's ark) and gathers into it his own family and male and female representatives of every living creature. When the flood comes, only those in the ark escape death. Gradually the waters subside and the survivors step out onto dry land once more, to begin to repopulate the earth.

The story is told in much more detail in the Bible and is made up of two different accounts so that some of the details do not fit. Any good story gets changed a little in the telling and many stories in the Bible were passed down by word of mouth for hundreds of years before being recorded in writing. So it is not surprising that there is sometimes more than one version of a story.

Assignments

15 Read the story of Noah's Ark from Genesis ch. 6 vv. 5—22, ch. 7 vv. 7—10 and 17—24, and ch. 8 vv. 6—17.

16 In this story, why did God decide to destroy everyone except Noah and his family?

17 What differences of detail can you spot between ch. 7 vv. 2—3 and ch. 6 v. 19; and also between ch. 7 v. 17 and ch. 7 v. 24?

We have said that myths are not concerned so much with history or science as with religious questions; but in 1929 a telegram arrived in England saying 'We have found the Flood.' It was from a British archaeologist named Sir Leonard Woolley, who was in charge of excavations in Iraq, at the ancient city of Ur. His team dug down to a thick layer of clay which showed that a flood had destroyed everything there in about 4000 BC. Woolley believed that the whole of this low-lying area of about 40,000 square miles was flooded at this time. The area was called Mesopotamia, a name which comes from two Greek words: *meso* meaning 'middle' and *potamis* meaning 'river'. It was the land between the twin rivers, the Tigris and the Euphrates, and was therefore prone to flooding. A very large flood would have seemed like a world disaster to the people of Mesopotamia, who were no doubt unaware of the existence of the rest of the world. So Woolley believed he had proved that the flood, referred to in the Bible, had actually happened.

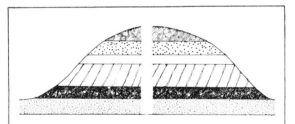

When a place has been lived in over many centuries, with people building on the remains of those who came before, gradually a mound (a 'tell') forms. Archaeologists dig a shaft through the middle of a tell. The layers, with different types of remains, show them how many civilisations lived there. A burnt layer would tell them that the buildings had been destroyed by fire, perhaps from enemy attack. A layer of mud would have been left by a flood.

Whether or not it was this very early flood, it is likely that a real flood did give rise to this story, as well as to other similar flood myths from Mesopotamia. The people of this region would have wondered why God let his creation be destroyed in this way. Myths may well reflect some historical situation, but their chief value is in their religious message. The Hebrews came to settle in Canaan, which is *not* subject to flooding, and yet they used this myth because its religious message was still relevant to them. It warned them of the dreadful consequences if they went their own way, ignoring the Maker's instructions on how to use his world.

The story ends with Noah offering a sacrifice to God to thank him for their deliverance. In return, God makes a covenant (a special agreement) with him. He promises never again to destroy the world in a flood, and gives Noah this sign by which to remember his promise:

> My bow I set in the cloud,
> sign of the covenant
> between myself and earth.
> When I cloud the sky over the earth,
> the bow shall be seen in the cloud.
> (Genesis ch. 9 vv. 13—14)

So the rainbow became the symbol of God's promise of mercy on his creation.

You can see how silly it becomes if you take this story *literally* rather than *symbolically*, and think that rainbows were given by God only after this great flood. Rainbows always form in the sky under certain conditions. These coloured arches are caused by the sun's rays being reflected off rain drops. So you should look for them whenever the sun is shining on a rainy day. The white rays of the sun are made up of six colours: red, orange, yellow, green, blue and purple. When the light bounces off a rain drop, these colours are separated out by being bent by different amounts, and a rainbow is formed. We now know the scientific explanation for rainbows, but this myth about the rainbow can still be true if we accept what it stands for: that God cares about the world he has created and will be merciful to it.

Assignments

18 Ask your science (physics) teacher to demonstrate how a ray of light can be shone through a prism to form a rainbow of colour. Or stand a glass of water on a flat sheet of white paper by a window, with the sun shining on it. You should see coloured light on the paper.
19 The rainbow is still a favourite symbol in stories. What are you supposed to find if you dig at the foot of a rainbow?

The story of Noah's Ark contains two very important Old Testament themes. The first is that of a faithful few who were saved by God from punishment and destruction, and from whom a godly people can grow. The second is the theme of the covenant, which sets the seal on a special relationship between God and people. Another word for covenant is 'testament'. You can now begin to see how important it is, for the two parts of the Christian Bible are called the Old and New Testaments.

The Tower of Babel, as imagined by an artist in the eighteenth century.

The Tower of Babel

This short myth in Genesis ch. 11 vv. 1—9 is another story of judgement. It tells how all human beings originally spoke a common language. Then they set to work and built themselves a city and 'a tower with its top in the heavens' because, we are told, they wanted to make a name for themselves. When God saw that they were getting above themselves, he confused their speech so that they had many languages, and he scattered them throughout the world.

We saw that the Flood myth probably grew up because of the actual experience of flooding in Mesopotamia. In the same way, it seems that this strange story of the tower has an historical explanation from the same area. Ancient people believed that God lived in the heavens up above them, so they thought that they were nearer to God on the top of a mountain and often built altars there. Mesopotamia is flat, low-lying ground, so the people there built artificial hills with terraced sides and a shrine at the very top for religious ceremonies. These temple-towers were called ziggurats, which meant 'mountain tops'. They symbolised stairways to heaven for the people of the plains. The remains of some of these ziggurats can still be seen in Mesopotamia today, over 4,000 years later.

Assignments

20 What feature can you often see on a church building which gives people the same idea of pointing up to heaven?

21 The image of heaven above us is still used today (e.g. the expression 'Heavens above!'). We often find this symbolism in poetry. Can you think of any lines or verses from hymns which are to do with God looking down on us from above?

22 We should not take literally this talk about heaven being a place up in the sky where God lives. It is picture-language. What ideas about God are expressed by talking in this way? (Think about how we use the image of someone being above or over us.)

Another obvious reason for the Tower of Babel myth is to explain why there are so many different languages in the world, just as the Flood myth gave an explanation for rainbows in pre-scientific times. The tower is called *Babel* both because it was in Babylon (a country of Mesopotamia) and because a similar Hebrew word meant 'confusion'. The foreign languages sounded just like *babble* to those who spoke a different language.

The editor of Genesis has taken over another ancient myth and fitted it into his framework of teaching. He has told us that God created a world good to live in, but that people were not satisfied with God's plans for order and unity. We have seen that Adam and Eve wanted to possess all knowledge, and that the people before the flood went their own way. God punished them for it, but people

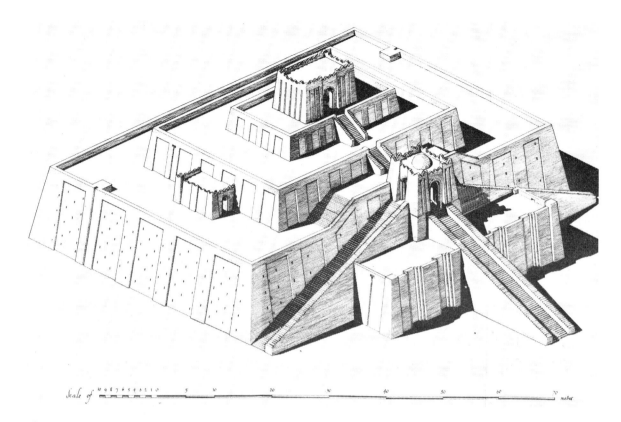

Scale of 10 9 8 7 6 5 4 3 2 1 0   5   10   20   30   40   50   60   70 metres

The ancient Babylonian city of Ur was excavated by Sir Leonard Woolley between 1922 and 1934. The photograph opposite shows how the ziggurat looked when it was first uncovered. Notice how this huge mound of solid brickwork towered above the rest of the site.

The ground floor of the ziggurat at Ur has now been restored so that tourists can climb to the top of the long flights of stairs just visible in the photograph.

The picture above shows what the ziggurat is believed to have looked like when it was first built.

had not yet learnt their lesson. Once more we have a story of people getting above their station, thinking they can arrange things better than God had done, and wanting to have more importance in the world. Yet again, the story is of God's judgement. In his anger, God now shatters the peace and order that he had created on earth, scattering people far and wide and making them foreigners to each other.

Assignment

23 Have you ever been in a situation where language was a barrier between you and another person? Discuss this in class, or write about one such experience.

The stories we have looked at so far say that this is God's world and he is in charge.

A song of praise to God the Creator of the world.

Psalm 150

O praise the LORD.

O praise God in his holy place,
praise him in the vault of heaven, the
    vault of his power;
praise him for his mighty works,
    praise him for his immeasurable
    greatness.
Praise him with fanfares on the trumpet,
    praise him upon lute and harp;
praise him with tambourines and dancing,
    praise him with flute and strings;
praise him with the clash of cymbals,
    praise him with triumphant cymbals;
let everything that has breath praise the
    LORD!

O praise the LORD.

1 Find a picture to stick into your exercise book, showing the beauty of the natural world. (You could cut out a picture from an old magazine, or use a photograph of your own.)
2 Think of one word to describe the photograph here.
3 Are there any aspects of the natural world which you find awe-inspiring, (which 'take your breath away')?
4 What about the cruel side of nature? Give some examples of this.
5 How can people still believe in a good God when faced with this other side of nature? Most Old Testament writers said it is our own fault. Do you think this is a good enough answer?

3 The Patriarchs

Genesis begins with myths about God, human beings and the world. They are timeless stories of long ago, set 'in the beginning' and 'once upon a time'. These myths concern all human beings. They show how people disobeyed God and brought disaster upon themselves. They end with the world thrown into confusion.

We now find our attention drawn to one particular individual who probably lived about 1800 BC. He was originally called Abram, but his name was changed to Abraham, which was understood to mean 'father of a multitude'; for he was the father of the people who were later called the Jews. The editor of Genesis has taken us right back to the earliest ancestor of the Jews, to show that God was guiding them from the beginning and shaping their destiny. But the story we are setting out on is not just the story of one small people. The Bible regards them as the People of God, through whom God would benefit the rest of the world. So we are now beginning the story of God's plan to save mankind.

Saga

With the story of Abraham we pass from the realm of myth to that of saga. A saga is the story of a family or tribe, told through the adventures of its folk-heroes and heroines, and passed down from one generation to another. Although they are historical in one sense, the stories have probably grown in the telling. Also, they concern themselves with private family affairs rather than with public or political incidents, so that it is difficult to

place them accurately in history. They may tell us things of historical interest, but cannot simply be called history. A saga does not have to be a religious story, but the sagas in Genesis have been set in a religious framework to unfold God's plan for his chosen people.

Assignment

1 Sagas often become popular television serials. Can you think of any and name the principal characters?

Abraham

The Abraham Saga takes up thirteen chapters of Genesis. We are told that he came from Harran in Mesopotamia. His father's tribe may have moved there from Ur, near the Persian Gulf, but the biblical text which records this is questionable. Abraham left his own country and migrated south with his close family and possessions to the land of Canaan (see map on page 31). There they lived as nomads, moving around to seek pasture for their herds of cattle and flocks of sheep and goats. Abraham eventually died in this land and was buried in Hebron.

Both Harran and Ur were centres of moon-worship, and yet Abraham came to worship God. His decision to part company with the rest of his father's tribe and travel into unknown territory is seen as a great act of faith in his new God:

Abraham and his family must have lived in tents like this, moving from place to place to find pasture for their sheep and goats, just as the Bedouin continue to do today in the same part of the world.

The LORD said to Abram, 'Leave your own country, your kinsmen, and your father's house, and go to a country that I will show you. I will make you into a great nation, I will bless you and make your name so great that it shall be used in blessings . . . And so Abram set out as the LORD had bidden him. (Genesis ch. 12 vv. 1—2 and 4)

This is showing us that, just as an act of disobedience had ruined mankind, so now an act of obedience was the first step in putting things right.

In the stories that follow, we see that Abraham came to know God more and more. God made a contract with him, called a covenant, in which he promised to give the land of Canaan to Abraham's descendants. A very ancient covenant ritual is preserved in this passage:

Abram said, 'O Lord GOD, how can I be sure that I shall occupy it?' The LORD answered, 'Bring me a heifer three years old, a she-goat three years old, a ram three years old, a turtle-dove, and a fledgling.' He brought him all these, halved the animals down the middle and placed each piece opposite its corresponding piece, but he did not halve the birds. (Genesis ch. 15 vv. 8—10)

At sunset, Abraham fell into a trance and he saw a vision of God passing between the carcass halves in the form of a smoking furnace and a flaming torch. In this way, God entered into a special relationship with Abraham and bound himself to keep his promise to him.

For his part, Abraham and all the men in his tribe were circumcised. The removal of the foreskin was a sign of the covenant, sealed in their flesh on the most private part of their bodies. Jews still perform this religious ritual today, on baby boys of eight days old. It symbolises their submission to God and is a daily reminder that they are the people of the covenant. They regard this as an important sign of loyalty to their religion.

Assignments

2 The meaning of ancient rituals is often difficult to interpret with certainty today. Why do *you* think God passed through the symbols of death when making the covenant with Abraham? Could it mean

that a person who breaks such a promise deserves to die? (Like the modern saying 'Cross my heart and hope to die.') What does the symbolism suggest to you?

3 Circumcision is a physical sign of being a Jew. Can you think of any other signs that people may have to remind themselves of their religion, especially things which affect their appearance (e.g. badges, clothes, hairstyles)?

Isaac

God had promised Abraham that he would be the father of many people, and yet Abraham's beautiful wife was childless. She was called Sarai, meaning Mockery, because it was a shameful thing in those days if a woman could not have children. Therefore, it was seen as a great blessing from God when at last, in her old age, Sarai became pregnant and had a baby boy, called Isaac. The proud mother was no longer called Sarai, but Sarah, which means princess!

You can imagine how Isaac grew up to be his father's pride and joy. All Abraham's hopes for his future descendants rested with Isaac, the only child of his marriage to Sarah. Then the day came when Abraham was asked to surrender the boy to God. The biblical account is a brilliant piece of story-telling which you must read for yourselves.

Assignments

4 a) Read Genesis ch. 22 vv. 1—13.
   b) Draw a picture-strip of the story.
5 Read the outcome of the incident in vv. 15—18.

The offering of human sacrifice has been practised at one time or another all over the world, because it is the supreme offering a person can make to God. This is particularly true where a child is to be the sacrifice, since a child is usually more precious to its parents than their own lives. No doubt, from his background, Abraham was used to this practice, and his devotion to God was so great that he was prepared to carry it out. He was prepared to give up the very thing that was most precious to him and upon which his hopes for the future were fixed. His faith passed the test, and God spared the child.

This story symbolises the rejection of human sacrifice in Old Testament times and the use of animal sacrifices instead, in the worship of God.

The story ends with Abraham finding a ram caught in a bush. This exquisite statue (of a he-goat rather than a ram) comes from the royal graves at Ur.

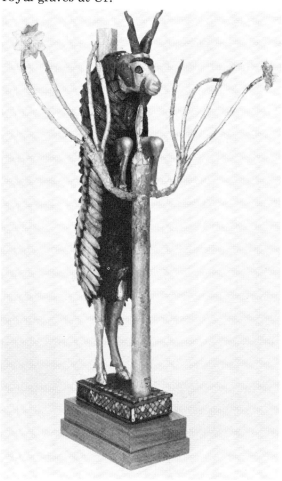

This was painted in the seventeenth century by the famous Dutch artist, Rembrandt, and one of his pupils. He knew the Bible stories in detail and made friends with the Jews in Amsterdam and visited their synagogues to try to learn more about their history. Which details of the story of Abraham's sacrifice does this picture show?

Assignments

6 Copy out this definition of sacrifice: *To make a sacrifice is to give up something very valuable to you, for the sake of something even more important.*

7 What was more important to Abraham than his son Isaac?

26

8 Why would it *not* be a sacrifice if you gave up something that you did not really want anyway?
9 What do *you* value most?

So Isaac was saved and grew to manhood. Abraham, his father, did not want him to marry a Canaanite woman, so he sent his servant back to his homeland to find Isaac a wife. Rebecca, Isaac's second cousin, was brought from Harran and she and Isaac were married.

After Abraham died, God renewed his promise, this time to Isaac:

> The LORD appeared to Isaac and said,' . . . Stay in this country and I will be with you and bless you, for to you and to your descendants I will give all these lands. Thus shall I fulfil the oath which I swore to your father Abraham. (Genesis ch. 26 vv. 2—3)

Jacob

Isaac and Rebecca had twin sons: Esau and Jacob. Although they were twins, Esau was the first-born and was considered to be the rightful heir. He grew up to be a strong, skilful hunter, fond of the outdoor life, and was his father's favourite. Jacob, on the other hand, was a quiet, home-loving boy who was closest to his mother.

Jacob may not have been the first-born, nor the strongest, but his story shows how he got to the top, and how the People of God were descended from him rather than Esau. As a young man, he made the most of opportunities and used persuasion and cunning to outwit both his brother and father. One day, when Esau was faint with hunger, he was persuaded to give up his birthright in exchange for a bowl of lentil soup! Then, when Isaac's eyesight was weak, and he thought he was close to death, he was misled into giving Jacob his blessing that he had meant for Esau. Not surprisingly, Esau bore a grudge against his brother and swore to kill him. Rebecca arranged for Jacob to escape, on the pretence of going back to Harran to find himself a wife.

Assignments

10 The story of how Jacob gained his father's blessing is in Genesis ch. 27 vv. 1—40.
   a) Get someone to read through this passage in the Bible, and then to tell the story to the rest of the class.
   b) Act out the story, with Isaac using the words of blessing from vv. 28—9.
11 A father's blessing was obviously very important in Jacob's day; and Jewish fathers still bless their children every Friday evening at the beginning of the Sabbath as shown in this photograph.

a) Who else, in our society, has the right to say a blessing over people?
b) What actions do they use to accompany their blessings?
c) Sometimes *things* are blessed rather than people. Can you think of any examples?
d) Why do you think we still have blessings today? Do they have any religious importance, or are they just tradition, or superstition?

On his way to Mesopotamia, Jacob slept one night out in the open and he had a memorable dream. It was of a ladder set up between heaven and earth, with angels going up and down on it. Then God spoke to Jacob:

> 'I am the LORD, the God of your father Abraham and the God of Isaac. This land on which you are lying I will give to you and your descendants. They shall be countless as the dust upon the earth, and you shall spread far and wide, to north and south, to east and west. . . . I will be with you, and I will protect you wherever you go and will bring you back to this land; for I will not leave you until I have done all that I have promised.' (Genesis ch. 28 vv. 13—15)

So the covenant relationship, established first of all with Abraham, was continued through Jacob. Jacob woke up in fear and trembling. Early the next morning he set up an altar to God there and poured onto it an offering of oil. We are told that the place was originally called Luz, but that Jacob renamed it Bethel, meaning 'House of God'.

Bethel was a very important religious centre for the Hebrews, but they had taken it over from the Canaanites. There may be traces of the Canaanite religion in this story. For instance, one of the ways of getting in touch with God was by sleeping at a sanctuary and having dreams which were interpreted by the temple staff. Also, their temples may have had a flight of steps leading up to the altar (as with the Babylonian ziggurats) which

could have led to the dream of a ladder reaching to heaven. The importance of the story was that no less a person than Jacob had declared the place to be a bethel, a 'house of God'. Therefore it must be all right for the Hebrews to worship there.

Another possibility is that the story grew up as an explanation of the place-name, Bethel. This was not uncommon.

Assignments

12 Look at a local map and pick out some interesting names of places. Try to discover any stories about their origins, or make up one for yourself.

13 Ancient people considered dreams to be important, but for a long time the scientific, Western world ignored them. Try to find out the names of the two great psychologists of this century who emphasised the importance of understanding dreams because they can bring to the surface what is going on deep down in our minds.

Jacob arrived safely in Harran and spent the next twenty years working for his Uncle Laban. He worked for fourteen years for the privilege of marrying Laban's two daughters: seven years for Leah and seven years for Rachel. This was a kind of dowry that he paid for them. He had only wanted to marry the younger daughter, Rachel, but their father thought it only proper for his elder daughter to be married first, and he tricked Jacob into it.

God did not appear to Jacob again during all these years, and yet the editor of the stories believed that God was still with him. When Jacob finally returned to Canaan he was an older and wiser man. They had been twenty difficult years but now Jacob had many possessions and a large family. The night before he crossed the river Jordan into Canaan, all the others had gone on ahead and Jacob was alone. There he met a stranger who wrestled with him all night:

> The man said, 'Let me go, for day is breaking', but Jacob replied, 'I will not let you go unless you bless me.' He said to Jacob, 'What is your name?', and he answered, 'Jacob.' The man said, 'Your name shall no longer be Jacob, but Israel, because you strove with God and with men, and prevailed.' (Genesis ch. 32 vv. 26–8)

So the symbolic name of Israel ('God strove') was given to Jacob, because he had come through the years of struggle and was now able to claim God's promise to give the land to him and his descendants. It was to be called the land of Israel, after him, and the twelve tribes of Israel were said to be descended from his twelve sons.

===

Assignments

14 Names are very important because they are symbolic. Your name is a symbol for you. It may have a further meaning, as in Giant Haystacks or Patience Strong; and it may have been chosen for you because your parents wanted you to be 'a little angel' (Angela) or to be lion-hearted (Leon), or whatever.
   a) Ask your parents why they chose your first names.
   b) Find out the meaning of at least one of your names. (If it comes from an ancient or foreign language, you may have to look it up in a dictionary of names.)
   c) If you could change one or other of your names, what would you change it to, and why?
   d) Can you think of any famous people who have names with an obvious meaning?
15 Jacob's name was changed to Israel. To change one's name is symbolic. It signifies a new start in life, a new relationship, or even a change of personality.
   a) When do women usually change their surnames?
   b) Can you think of types of religious people who take on new names at important moments in their lives?
   c) Can you remember the original names of Abraham and Sarah? (see pages 23 and 25)
   d) What does Sarah mean? (see page 25)

===

Joseph

The story of 'Israel' ends, not in the land which was named after him, but in Egypt. How this comes about is explained in the Joseph Story, a long and colourful story which fills a quarter of the book of Genesis. It is written in the form of a popular romance, with a theme found in many other folk-tales: how a poor boy makes good. Joseph is sold into slavery in Egypt, but rises to become second only to the Pharaoh himself.

The Joseph Story shows us that God was still guiding his people, even when it looked as though disaster had overtaken them. Israel's tribe was faced with starvation in Canaan at a time of severe drought but, through a twist of fate, Joseph was already powerful in Egypt so that they were welcome to settle there. This long story contains very few details from which we can set it precisely within history. It has been suggested that the Hebrews might have been tolerated in Egypt by the Hyksos rulers (*c.* 1720–1570 BC) since they were both of the same Semitic race. If so, it could be that when the Hyksos were expelled, the Children of Israel were also unwelcome and were badly treated.

The editor of the Pentateuch also uses this story to make the link between the stories of the early fathers of the Jews in Canaan and the stories of Moses in Egypt. So the stage is set for Moses, the next great hero, to lead them out of Egypt and back to the Promised Land.

===

Assignments

16 Who was Joseph? (see the *History Chart* on page 7)

17 Read Psalm 105 vv. 16—23, which gives a summary of the Joseph Story and shows that it was all seen to be part of God's plan for his chosen people.

18 Perhaps you could listen to some songs from the musical, *Joseph and the Amazing Technicolor Dreamcoat.*

19 Can you name any fairy-tales which also have the theme of a poor boy who rises to fame and fortune?

'Joseph makes himself known to his Brethren.' This is a late nineteenth-century engraving. Notice how the artist has tried to show Egyptian decorations in the building and in Joseph's head-dress, in contrast with the Hebrew costumes of his brothers. Do you know what the two Egyptian figures on the left are called, each with a lion's body and a human head?

The 'Fertile Crescent' refers to the arc of low-lying, well-watered land stretching from Babylon to Canaan (although the fertile area extends on into the Nile delta in Egypt). This was the most populated area since the rest was mountains and deserts.

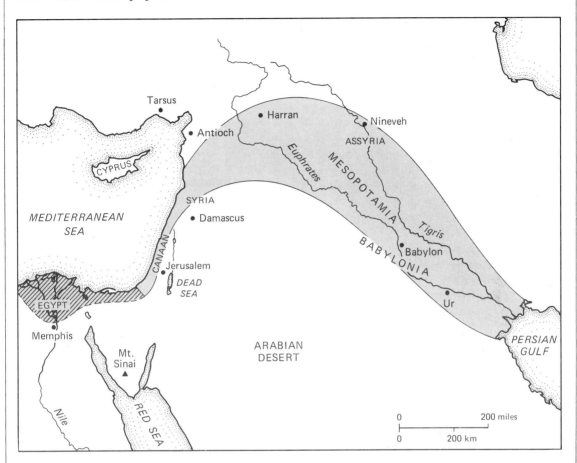

1 Find Harran where Abraham came from, where Rebecca was brought from and where Jacob spent twenty years with his uncle Laban.
2 Which was the land that was promised to Abraham and his descendants? (Use the name on the map.)

3 Which two rivers flow through Mesopotamia? What does the name 'Mesopotamia' mean? (see page 18) This area was prone to flooding and gave rise to the Flood myths.
4 Notice where Egypt, Syria, Assyria and Babylon are. These great powers all ruled empires in their time, which extended into Canaan.

After the Conquest, the 'Promised Land' was mainly called **Israel** in the Bible. This was in the ancient land of **Canaan** and Philistia (the thin coastal strip where the Philistines lived). From the first century AD the name Philistia became **Palestine** and was used for this whole region.

We call the 'People of God' **Hebrews** in the early stages; then the **Children of Israel** or **Israelites** during the monarchy; and then **Jews** from the sixth century onwards.

4 Moses

Epic

You may be used to the term 'epic' to describe a certain type of film at the cinema or on the television. An epic is a long, continuous story, telling the achievements of a great hero, or a group of heroes. The heroes may come from our distant past, but they are still remembered because they helped make us the people that we are today. The heroes were real, historical characters who did great things, but the epics, written in praise of them, are exaggerated. This does not mean they are dishonest or misleading. By embroidering the stories, an epic presents us with the truth about the hero's greatness, as the writers saw it. In so doing, they arouse our admiration for all the good things the hero stood for.

Moses is the hero in the next stage of the Old Testament story of the People of God. It was he who freed them from slavery in Egypt, taught them about God, ruled over them for many years in the wilderness and led them towards the Promised Land. He is known as a leader, teacher, law-giver and prophet (a spokesman for God). The figure of Moses strides through the last four books of the Pentateuch; and Jews call this first, most important section of the Old Testament the 'Five Books of Moses'. The Pentateuch ends with these words:

> There has never yet risen in Israel a prophet like Moses, whom the LORD knew face to face: remember all the signs and portents which the LORD sent him to show in Egypt to Pharaoh and all his servants and the whole land; remember the strong hand of Moses and the terrible deeds which he did in the sight of all Israel. (Deuteronomy ch. 34 vv. 10—12)

You can imagine the epic of Moses, brought to the screen in glorious technicolor.

Assignment

1 Name some epics that have been made into films (e.g. *Ben Hur*).

Moses in the Bulrushes

Moses did not become the leader of the Hebrews until he was well on in years; and yet we begin with his birth-story. The story is a spectacular one, following a theme which can be found in folk-tales: that of a baby, rescued by a princess and brought up in a palace. Indeed, the story of Moses in the Bulrushes is very similar to the birth-story of Sargon, the great hero of the ancient Akkadians, who lived many centuries before Moses (c. 2500 BC). Sargon claimed that his mother had put him into a river in a water-proof basket made from rushes, from where he was rescued.

We cannot say how much historical truth there is in the story of Moses' birth. At least the fact that he had been connected with the Egyptians (as seen in his Egyptian name) is unlikely to have been made up by the Hebrews, for the Egyptians were their enemies. Whatever the historical basis of this story, it certainly has symbolic value. It tells us that God had chosen Moses for a special purpose from the very beginning of his life.

God had saved Moses from death and planned his upbringing so that he kept his ties with his Hebrew family whilst also gaining all the benefits of an adopted Egyptian prince. Moses was obviously being shaped for his future task when, as leader of his own people, the Hebrews, he would have to stand up to Pharaoh himself (the Egyptian king).

Assignments

2 Read the background explanation to Moses' birth-story in Exodus ch. 1 vv. 6—22.
   a) Why did the new Pharaoh fear the Hebrew immigrants? (vv. 9—10)
   b) What work were the Hebrew slaves made to do? (vv. 11 and 14)
   c) What did Pharaoh want the midwives to do? (v. 16)
   d) What did Pharaoh finally resort to? (v. 22)
3 Read the story of Moses in the Bulrushes in Exodus ch. 2 vv. 1—10; and write an account of what happened as though you were Moses' sister (Miriam).

The burning bush

When Moses grew up, he was forced to flee from Egypt because he had killed an Egyptian taskmaster who was flogging a Hebrew slave. Moses travelled east and settled with the Midianites. There he became a shepherd, married a priest's daughter and had a family. Moses may well have got many of his religious ideas from Jethro, his father-in-law.

One day, when Moses was taking his sheep to find pasture, he came to a mountain which was to become very holy in Hebrew traditions. In some traditions it is called Mount Sinai, and in others, Mount Horeb. It is not known for sure where this mountain is. It is claimed to be Jebel Musa, a mountain near the tip of the Sinai Peninsula which rises to 2285 m (see p. 39). On the holy mountain, Moses had an experience of meeting with God and being called to lead God's people to freedom.

We are told that God spoke to Moses from a burning bush, a bush which appeared to be on fire and yet was not being burnt up. There may be some natural explanation for this, but it was unusual enough to catch Moses' eye. Any unusual appearance of fire was understood as a symbol of God's presence, so that Moses would have been ready for a religious experience.

As Moses approached the burning bush, God called to him:

'Come no nearer; take off your sandals; the place where you are standing is holy ground.' (Exodus ch. 3 v. 5).

Moses felt afraid. You will know something of how he felt if you can imagine coming across an electric generator, surrounded by high barbed-wire fencing and padlocked gates. A notice in large red letters says: 'Danger. Keep out.' You know that there is something powerful and dangerous there which you do not fully understand. It is a little bit frightening and you have to take care. Moses took off his shoes as a sign of reverence, to show that this was no ordinary place for him.

Assignments

4 Can you remember how God was symbolised when he made the covenant with Abraham? (see page 24)
5 Look up Exodus ch. 13 v. 21 to find out what symbol represented God's presence as he led the Hebrews through the wilderness by night.
6 No doubt it is because fire is powerful and sometimes frightening that it has become a symbol for God. Is there anything else about fire which you could also say about God?
7 Do you know of any religions which still insist that you take off your shoes in their places of worship?
8 What else might people do today, apart from removing their shoes, to show that they are in a holy place?
9 Have you ever felt a sense of awe in a particular place or in someone's presence? If you do not mind sharing your experience, try to write a description of it.
10 Read Exodus ch. 3 vv. 1—6.

The name of God

God told Moses that he wanted him to rescue his people from Egypt and Moses asked God to tell him his name:

> Then Moses said to God, 'If I go to the Israelites and tell them that the God of their forefathers has sent me to them, and they ask me his name, what shall I say?' God answered, 'I AM; that is who I am. Tell them that I AM has sent you to them.' And God said further, 'You must tell the Israelites this, that it is JEHOVAH the God of their forefathers, the God of Abraham, the God of Isaac, the God of Jacob, who has sent you to them. This is my name for ever; this is my title in every generation.' (Exodus ch. 3 vv. 13—15)

Even an ordinary person's name is important. It is something personal which you do not disclose to just anybody. Only those reasonably close to you will use your first name; and you may have a nickname that only your family or friends know. So by telling Moses his name, God was showing that Moses and the Hebrews were in a close relationship with him.

More than that, Moses was asking God to tell him about his nature; and that is what God did, for the name he gave was symbolic. It came from the verb 'to be' and is difficult to translate into English. It probably means that God is the source of all life, that he is the living God who has always existed and always will exist.

The Hebrew name of God.
We do not really know how this should be pronounced. Jews consider God's name to be so holy that they never say it and the Hebrew alphabet has no vowels. The N.E.B. translates it as 'Jehovah' but most scholars think that 'Yahweh' is more accurate.

The Exodus

The most important event in Moses' career was the Exodus ('going out'), when he led the Hebrews out of Egypt. The book of Exodus is named after this.

The plight of the Hebrew slaves obviously worried Moses, even after years of separation from them, and he now believed that God wanted him to go back to Egypt, to save them. So he travelled back to Egypt and asked Pharaoh to let God's people go. At first Pharaoh refused, until a series of plagues, ending with the death of the first-born, caused him to beg the Hebrews to leave. Moses had made sure that they were all packed and ready to go.

After a while, however, Pharaoh changed his mind and led his army out in pursuit of

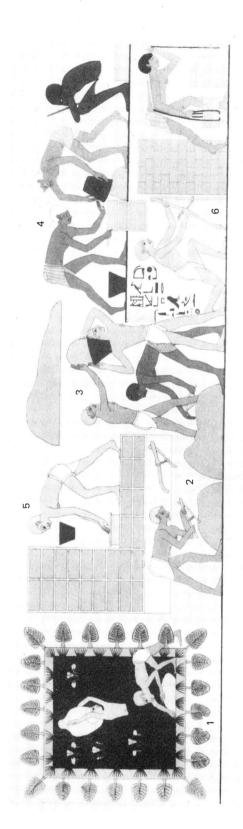

This was one long wall-painting from an Egyptian tomb of the Eighteenth Dynasty (about 1550—1350 BC). It shows slaves making bricks, just as the Hebrews did for Pharaoh. Can you spot the two Egyptian taskmasters?

1. Drawing water 2. Mixing the wet clay 3. Carrying it in buckets 4. Making the bricks in moulds 5. Drying them in the sun 6. Stacking them 7. Carrying them away.

the runaway slaves. At the Sea of Reeds, a strong east wind was blowing. This meant that the Hebrews were able to get across on dry land; but when the Egyptians tried to cross in their chariots, the wheels got bogged down in the mud, and the Hebrews made good their escape. We do not know where this sea was (it is not the Red Sea, which is a wrong translation), but there are a number of possible lakes which had shallows that people could walk through.

It is interesting to notice that only the later strand of this story exaggerates the miraculous crossing by having Moses stretching out his magic rod over the sea, and the waters dividing into walls between which the Hebrews passed, but which crashed down and drowned the Egyptians. The earlier strand of the story is easier to accept, but the later details show us how the people came to understand this incident. It was for them no coincidence, but a great miracle. God had saved them from their enemies. This was seen as yet another example of how God was guiding his people.

Assignments

11 Exodus ch. 15 is a song of triumph over the defeat of the Egyptians. Either read it all through, or just read vv. 1—2 and 13.
12 Imagine you are among those who have escaped from Egypt. Write an entry in your diary about this incident at the Sea of Reeds.

The Passover

The editor of the Pentateuch has linked the story of Moses with that of the forefathers of the Hebrews; but really it was a new beginning. Just as Abraham was called out of Mesopotamia and led to the Promised Land, so now the Hebrews are called out of Egypt and led there under Moses. The Exodus is presented as the supreme moment when God acted in history to save his chosen people. For their part, the people accepted God as their God and agreed to worship him alone

and to live by his laws. Many basic Jewish beliefs and practices go back to this time.

One of the most ancient passages in the Bible, recited by the Hebrews as they brought their gifts at Harvest Festival, shows us that the Exodus was the chief reason for regarding themselves as the chosen people of God:

'My father was a homeless [or wandering] Aramaean who went down to Egypt with a small company and lived there until they became a great, powerful, and numerous nation. But the Egyptians ill-treated us, humiliated us and imposed cruel slavery upon us. Then we cried to the LORD the God of our fathers for help, and he listened to us and saw our humiliation, our hardship and distress; and so the LORD brought us out of Egypt with a strong hand and outstretched arm, with terrifying deeds, and with signs and portents. He brought us to this place and gave us this land, a land flowing with milk and honey.' (Deuteronomy ch. 26 vv. 5—9)

So important was the Exodus in the history of the People of God that, even today, Jews remember this great event every year at the Passover Festival. They relive the story of the Exodus as though they themselves were there, for each Jew still has a strong sense of belonging to the chosen people, and still believes in God as one who frees people from oppression. During the week of Passover they eat only unleavened bread, to remember their ancestors who left Egypt in such a hurry that they did not have time to wait for the dough to rise. At the Passover supper they eat symbolic foods to illustrate the story of the Exodus: bitter herbs for the bitter suffering of the Hebrews in slavery; dipped in salt-water to represent their tears of sorrow; a sweet mixture of nuts and apple to symbolise the cement used in their slave-labour; and so on.

The Passover is probably the most ancient of the Jewish festivals, although the rules given for it in Exodus chapter 12 come from the Priestly writers a long time after the Exodus itself.

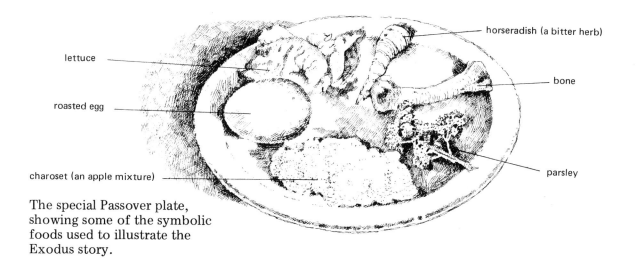

lettuce

horseradish (a bitter herb)

roasted egg

bone

charoset (an apple mixture)

parsley

The special Passover plate, showing some of the symbolic foods used to illustrate the Exodus story.

Assignments

13 Copy out Deuteronomy ch. 26 vv. 8—9.
14 Find out more about the Jewish Passover, particularly the symbolic foods. (Look up a textbook on Judaism.)

This Jewish family is celebrating the special Passover meal. The father is leading the ceremony by reading the story of the Exodus.

The Covenant

Some time after escaping from Egypt, they reached Mount Sinai (or Mount Horeb) where God had first met with Moses. God appeared there once again. Through Moses, he gave the people the chance to enter into a special agreement with him, called a covenant. We have seen that God made covenants with Abraham, Isaac and Jacob but this Mosaic Covenant (i.e. under Moses) was made with the whole people. God promised that he would treat them as his special people, and they agreed to keep the laws of the covenant, summed up in the Ten Commandments.

Because the mountain was thought to be such a holy place, Moses had a barrier put round it to stop people touching it. They were to keep a respectful distance. They kept themselves clean for three days so that they would be worthy of God's presence among them. We are told that God's arrival was heralded by 'peals of thunder and flashes of lightning', 'dense cloud' and smoking fire. This description might suggest that a volcano was erupting, or at least a violent storm. Primitive people, who did not understand the natural causes of these things, might have believed that they were signs of God's activity on the mountain. However, we have already seen that fire was a symbol for God's presence, especially in unusual or very powerful forms. So whether or not fire blazed from Mount Sinai, this description is a way of emphasising, in picture-language, the awareness at that time of God's all-powerful and all-holy presence.

We are also told that there was a dense cloud on the top of the mountain, and this too was a symbol for God's presence. It comes from the idea that God is too great for people to set eyes upon him, and therefore a cloud veils him from sight.

Assignments

15 Read Deuteronomy ch. 11 vv. 26—8 which explains the two sides of the Mosaic Covenant.
16 In some church buildings there is a place which is regarded as especially holy, where only priests and servers may go during the services. Which part of the church is this and what happens there?
17 Look up Exodus ch. 13. v. 21 again, to find out what symbol represented God's presence as he led the Hebrews through the wilderness by day.

The Ten Commandments

There are 613 laws altogether in the Pentateuch, but they are all summed up in the Ten Commandments. This was the law-code with which Moses ruled the people. He is said to have received it from God on Mount Sinai and brought it to the people inscribed on two pillars of stone. These were kept in a box, specially made for the purpose, called the Ark of the Covenant. The first four of the Ten Commandments deal with religious beliefs and practices, and the last six with how God wanted his people to treat one another.

The God of the Ten Commandments was a God who acted in history to save his chosen people from their enemies. He was to be the only God for the Hebrews. He could not be portrayed in human images, for he was so much greater than the human mind could imagine. He was a holy God who had to be respected. He was a moral God who wanted his people to be good: to respect people's lives, property and families. He was a just God who punished the wicked and rewarded the righteous.

Assignment

18 Read Exodus ch. 20 vv. 1—17 and make a list of the Ten Commandments. The first four are: (1) You shall have no other God to set against me (v. 3). (2) You shall not make a carved image . . . you shall not worship them (vv. 4—6). (3) You shall not misuse God's name (v. 7). (4) Keep the sabbath day holy (vv. 8—11).

We are told that the Wilderness Period lasted for 40 years. This was a 'round figure', as 10, 50, 100 or 1,000 might be for us. It signified a generation. It was a time of many hardships for the Hebrews, but a time when they were being knocked into shape as the People of God. Under Moses' leadership they survived and came to know God. Moses finally died, at a ripe old age, on Mount Nebo, overlooking the blue waters of the Dead Sea to the Promised Land beyond.

Jebel (Mount) Musa. This is claimed to be Mount Sinai where God met with Moses in the burning-bush incident and where the Mosaic Covenant was made. Moses is said to have come down from the mountain carrying the stone tablets on which the Ten Commandments were inscribed.

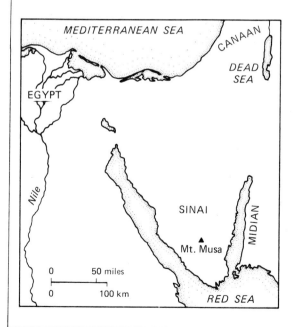

1 Find Musa on the map.
2 What is the other name the Bible uses for Mount Sinai? (see page 33)
3 Read Exodus ch. 19 vv. 17—20 and paint a picture of the scene it conjures up for you.
4 Another important meeting with God took place on this mountain. Read I Kings ch. 19 vv. 8—14. To whom did God speak on this occasion?
5 Have you ever stood on the top of a mountain, either with a clear view, or with your head in the clouds? Write a few sentences describing how you felt.
6 Ancient people often thought their gods lived on the tops of mountains. What do you think led them to believe this?

5 In the Promised Land

Joshua

Moses' successor was Joshua, his right-hand man and a faithful worshipper of God:

> Moses summoned Joshua and said to him in the presence of all Israel, 'Be strong, be resolute; for it is you who are to lead this people into the land which the Lord swore to give their forefathers, and you are to bring them into possession of it. The Lord himself goes at your head; he will be with you; he will not fail you or forsake you. Do not be discouraged or afraid.' (Deuteronomy ch. 31 vv. 7—8)

The story of Joshua is told in the book named after him, where we are given a picture of a great commander at the head of his troops, conquering the Canaanite cities and taking the land for the People of God. After the miraculous fall of Jericho, three quick wars seem to have brought all Canaan under

his control. Then Joshua divided the land between the twelve tribes of Israel.

Yet when we look at all the information more carefully, we learn that the conquest of Canaan was far more difficult than this and was not fully completed at this time. It is more likely that the Hebrew tribes gradually took possession of the land: sometimes making treaties with those who were friendly; sometimes having to fight for it; and usually settling in the less fertile hill-country where there were not many people to deal with.

Simple trumpets made from rams' horns are still used by Jews today. They are blown on special occasions in their synagogues.

Assignments

1 Read Joshua ch. 6 vv. 1—21 and write a paragraph to describe the fall of Jericho. (You may find it difficult to work out the details exactly because two different versions of the story have been woven together. In one, the procession was in silence until the final war cry when 'the walls came tumbling down'. In the other, the priests went before the holy Ark, blowing their trumpets of rams' horns.)

2 If you were a Jew, listening to the story of the fall of Jericho, would you think it was just an interesting piece of history, or would you see some signs in it that God was on your side? If so, what are they?

Sacred history

There is a long farewell speech of Joshua's when he was old and near to death. Such speeches were used by the biblical writers to sum up the importance of a hero's life. In this speech we see the lesson that the writers are to draw out again and again in the period of history that they are covering. The lesson is that God kept the covenant with his people: he supported them in battle when they kept his laws, but punished them when they disobeyed and worshipped other gods, giving them into the hands of their enemies.

Jericho (left) is the earliest known fortified city in the world, with remains of stone walls dating back to about 7000 BC. It may well be the earliest place that people ever settled in. The ancient site of Jericho has been discovered in a mound beside the modern city of the same name, 30 km N.E. of Jerusalem. Restaurants in modern Jericho issue certificates to say that you have dined at the lowest spot on the earth's surface, for Jericho is 250 metres below sea-level. It is in the Jordan valley — a great rift in the earth's crust, running north—south through Palestine. This area is prone to earthquakes which have destroyed buildings there; and there have been a series of cities built on the ancient site. This photograph shows the Western Entrance to Jericho. This ancient roadway leads to two narrow gateways into the city which stood there several centuries before the time of Joshua.

This lesson was very important to these writers who were looking back over about 600 years of their history. The high spots for them were when God had given them the land, the monarchy and the temple; but they were writing at the time of the Exile, when all these things were taken from them (see the *History Chart* on page 7). Somehow they had to make sense of all this. Their answer came from their understanding of the covenant:

Understand that this day I offer you the choice of a blessing and a curse. The blessing will come if you listen to the commandments of the LORD your God which I give you this day, and the curse if you do not listen to the commandments of the LORD your God but turn aside from the way that I command you this day and follow other gods whom you do not know. (Deuteronomy ch. 11 vv. 26—8)

So although they were recording history, it was history with a particular religious purpose, which we can call sacred history.

Assignment

3 In Joshua's speech (Joshua ch.23), the attitude of the writers is very clear. Read the verses in brackets to answer the following questions:
   a) Who had fought for the Hebrews and given them victory? (vv. 1—3)
   b) What had God given to his people? (vv. 4—5)
   c) How should the people respond to God? (v. 6)
   d) What should they avoid doing? (vv. 7—8)
   e) What threat is held over them? (v. 15)
   f) What would the people have to do for this threat to come true? (v. 16)

Judges

After the Conquest under Joshua came the Settlement Period when each Hebrew tribe settled down to manage its own affairs. The book which covers this period is called Judges. The judges were not the type we are used to, sitting in law-courts and wearing long, white wigs. The 'judges' of the Hebrews were more like army generals. Even today, in troubled parts of the world, we sometimes hear of army commanders taking over the country during a crisis and ruling for some time afterwards. Similarly, when a Hebrew tribe was in danger from surrounding Canaanite tribes, then a great military leader would emerge, known as a 'judge'.

The writers saw a clear pattern in the history of the judges, in line with their belief that God rewarded the faithful and punished those who disobeyed the covenant laws. They presented the story of each judge in this neat pattern:
   i) The people started to worship the Canaanite gods and goddesses (e.g. the Baalim and the Asheroth).
   ii) God no longer gave them victory over their enemies.
   iii) They repented and cried to God for help.
   iv) God raised up a judge among them who saved them from their enemies.
   v) The judge kept them faithful to God for the rest of his/her life.
Then the people strayed from God again and the pattern kept repeating itself.

This pattern can be seen very clearly in the story of the first judge, whose name was Othniel:

[i] The Israelites did what was wrong in the eyes of the LORD; they forgot the LORD their God and worshipped the Baalim and the Asheroth. [ii] The Lord was angry with Israel and he sold them to C . . . , who kept them in subjection for eight years. [iii] Then the Israelites cried to the LORD for help [iv] and he raised up a man to deliver them, Othniel . . . , and he set them free. The spirit of the LORD came upon him and he became judge over Israel. He took the field, and the LORD delivered C . . . into his hands; Othniel was too strong for him. [v] Thus the land was at peace for forty years until Othniel son of Kenaz died. (Judges ch. 3 vv. 7—11)

Assignments

4 What happened after Othniel died? (see Judges ch. 3 vv. 12—14)
5 Find out the names of two of the most famous judges, in Judges ch. 4 v. 4 and ch. 6 v. 34.

It was the Assyrians who conquered the northern kingdom of Israel. This scene shows them attacking a walled city (like the capital of Israel). You can see some Assyrian infantrymen, a battering-ram and their enemies impaled on stakes in the background.

The monarchy

By the middle of the twelfth century BC an even more dangerous enemy than the Canaanites had arrived on the scene: the powerful Philistines. The Hebrews realised that they could no longer survive in separate tribes, but would have to unite under one permanent leader and have a regular army. Saul became the first king but it was David, his successor, who really made his mark on the kingship.

The writers of Joshua and Judges also wrote the books of Samuel and Kings. David was clearly their great hero, and all the kings who were descended from him were judged to be good or bad depending on how well they followed in his footsteps. After the reign of his son, Solomon, the kingdom split into two and David's descendants only ruled the southern kingdom of Judah (see map on page 58). The northern kings of Israel were all condemned by these historians for breaking away.

The importance of David comes across even more strongly in the writings of another biblical historian, in the books of I and II Chronicles, Ezra and Nehemiah. When the Chronicler wrote up the same history of the monarchy, he concentrated entirely on the southern kingdom, and devoted most chapters to David and Solomon, in whose reign the temple was built.

The writers of these sacred histories believed that David had been a righteous king who was faithful to God. Looking back, they must have thought: 'If only all our kings had been like King David, and we had remained faithful to God, worshipping under the king's guidance in the Jerusalem temple — then none of these disasters would have happened to us.'

This is the comment of our previous writers on the fall of the northern kingdom of Israel in 722 BC:

> All this happened to the Israelites because they had sinned against the LORD their God who brought them up from Egypt, from the rule of Pharaoh king of Egypt; they paid homage to other gods . . .
> (II Kings ch. 17 v 7)

In due course, the southern kingdom of Judah also collapsed and, once more, the writers of this sacred history saw a religious lesson in it:

> Even Judah did not keep the commandments of the LORD their God but followed the practices adopted by Israel; so the LORD rejected the whole race of Israel and punished them and gave them over to plunderers and finally flung them out of his sight. (II Kings ch. 17 vv. 19—20)

Assignment

6 The idea of punishment or blessing is a *religious* way of interpreting history. How might you describe the events of this chapter if you do not have a belief in God?

Unscramble the letters to check your answers to the following questions.
1 Which king was the hero of the Deuteronomic historians and the Chronicler? ADDIV
2 Who took over from Moses? AUSHOJ
3 Which city was the first major obstacle in Canaan? ERICJOH
4 What were the Hebrew leaders called who arose in times of trouble? UGSEDJ
5 Who were the greatest enemies of the Hebrews at this time? HISTINPILES
6 Who was the first Hebrew king? LAUS
7 After the division of the kingdom, what was the northern kingdom called? RAELIS
8 What was the southern kingdom called? DUHAJ
9 Where was the temple of God? EMASRUJEL
10 Where were the Jews taken into Exile? NOLBABY

6 David

David was the greatest king the Israelites ever had. He put down the Philistines and other surrounding enemies, and set himself up in Jerusalem from where he controlled a great empire. After him, his descendants ruled over the southern kingdom of Judah for 400 years.

David was so successful that he became a legendary hero in the history of the Jews. Stories were told about him to emphasise his good qualities of courage and faithfulness to God. The whole of the book of Psalms came to be attributed to him in tradition. He was even seen as the model for the future saviour, the Messiah, who was called the Son of David. David must have made a very big impact for such legends to have grown up around him, and they are true in so far as they witness to his greatness. But we cannot be sure that they all actually happened. They are not history, although David himself was a real, historical figure and the legends have some historical basis.

On the other hand, there is one section of the story of David in the books of Samuel which *can* be regarded as history. It is known as the Court History (II Samuel chapters 9—20 and I Kings chapters 1—2) and seems to have been written soon after the events it records, by someone from the royal court who knew David personally. This section sheds a new light on David. Here his public image is shattered by glimpses of his personal life which involved adultery, murder and family intrigue and rebellion. It is interesting that the Chronicler omits this section of David's life.

We might construct a more accurate picture of David by a cold, historical approach, but the legends are symbolic stories which show us the meaning that he held for the people of Judah.

Assignment

1 The emblem of the Jews since the Middle Ages is known as the 'Star of David' (or, more correctly, the 'Shield of David').
   a) Learn how to draw it.
   b) Do you know where you would see this emblem today?

David's anointing

We first meet David in the story of his anointing by Samuel the prophet. Samuel felt led by God to Bethlehem to anoint one of the sons of Jesse to be the future king. Samuel invited Jesse and his sons to a religious ceremony and there he inspected them, starting with the eldest son. As each one came before him, he felt sure that this must be the one, but each time God rejected him, until all seven sons had passed before Samuel. The prophet asked if there were any more, and he was told of David, the youngest, who was out minding the sheep. Samuel asked for him to be brought, and when he set eyes upon him he knew immediately that this was the Lord's anointed. David was a very handsome youth, with tanned skin and bright eyes. Samuel anointed him to be the next king of Israel by pouring over his head the oil which he had brought for the purpose.

This story was probably added later to the whole account of David because it fits awkwardly with the description of David that follows. There he is said to be a skilful soldier who was appointed to play the lyre to Saul when he was depressed; although it does say that he was brought from minding the sheep, to make the connection with the previous story. The anointing also contains the 'Cinderella' theme of the youngest and least likely being chosen for great things.

Assignment

2 We are told that David was handsome, as befits a crown prince. In fairy stories good people are often symbolised as beautiful, and bad people as ugly. Discuss if this is still true in modern stories and films.

David and Goliath

The next story, of David and Goliath, is even more famous. It tells how the Philistines had challenged the Israelites to face Goliath of Gath in single combat. He was a giant of a man and the sight of him, clad in his heavy armour, struck fear into the hearts of the Israelite soldiers, and no one could be found to stand up to him. Then David, the shepherd boy, arrived to bring supplies from home to his older brothers. When he heard about Goliath he was keen to go out to fight him, declaring:

> 'The LORD who saved me from the lion and the bear will save me from this Philistine.' (I Samuel ch. 17 v. 37)

King Saul tried to arm this reckless youth, but David preferred a stout stick and his sling and stones. 'Am I a dog', asked Goliath, 'that you come out against me with sticks?' But David replied:

> 'You have come against me with sword and spear and dagger, but I have come against you in the name of the LORD of Hosts, the God of the army of Israel which you have defied. The LORD will put you into my power this day; I will kill you and cut your head off and leave your carcass and the carcasses of the Philistines to the birds and wild beasts.' (I Samuel ch. 17 vv. 45—6)

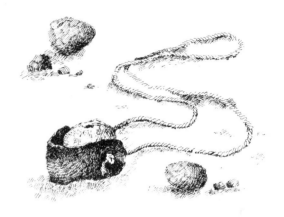

And that is precisely what David did. He killed Goliath with a stone carefully aimed at his forehead. When the Philistines saw that their champion was dead they ran away, but the Israelites pursued them and won a great victory. David remained in Saul's army and did many more heroic deeds.

Historians have many reasons to doubt the historical accuracy of this story. Just before this we are told that David had entered Saul's service and been appointed as his personal armour bearer. Yet at the end of this story we

A statue of David (right) by the Italian artist and sculptor Bernini (1598—1680). It is actually a self-portrait. In order to make the moment when David attacked Goliath as lifelike as possible, Bernini pulled a face in a mirror and copied that. What do you think lies at David's feet? (see I Samuel ch. 17 vv. 38—9)

LXXVII

are told that David was presented to King Saul and he asked him who he was. It also mentions that David took Goliath's head to Jerusalem, yet Jerusalem was still a foreign city at that time. Furthermore, we read elsewhere that:

> Elhanan son of Jair of Bethlehem killed Goliath of Gath, whose spear had a shaft like a weaver's beam. (II Samuel ch. 21 v. 19)

So perhaps this victory was attributed to David when he became king and supreme commander of the army; just as we might say that a king had won the victories during his reign.

Whatever historical battles with the Philistines lie behind this story, it is clear that it is a legend whose purpose was to heighten David's reputation as a great warrior, by attributing such a heroic act to him when he was still little more than a boy. Also, David represents the whole of Israel, a young nation pitted against mighty enemies, but assured of victory in the name of the Lord. It also assures us that goodness can overcome evil, however unfavourable the odds may appear.

Assignments

3 Read the story of David and Goliath in I Samuel ch. 17, and then mime it.
4 Draw or paint a picture of Goliath (described in I Samuel ch. 17 vv. 4—7); or do a picture of a purely imaginary giant.

David's success as a soldier led Saul to insane jealousy of him and a number of attempts on his life. David was forced to flee into exile where he became a 'Robin Hood' figure with his band of outlaws. During those years, David got into many scrapes but managed to avoid wrong-doing and to turn every situation to his own advantage.

The book of I Samuel ends on a sad note with the death of Saul in battle and the Israelites in defeat. David was seen as the obvious choice of king in the south, but it was another seven years before he was accepted by the north as well. He captured Jerusalem from the Canaanites and made it his capital city from where he governed both political and religious matters. He established the Ark of the Covenant in Jerusalem and bought the land on which the temple was later built, in the reign of his son, Solomon. The southern writers record that God made a special covenant with David which guaranteed that his dynasty would survive for ever. God would punish evil kings but he would never totally destroy the house of David.

This idea is illustrated in the Court History which follows soon after the chapter on the Davidic Covenant (II Samuel ch. 7). It is now that we see the other side of David; but even though he committed grave sins, God was still prepared to forgive him when David was sorry for them.

David was staying in the royal city of Jerusalem while his army was away on a campaign. As he strolled on the flat roof of his palace in the cool of the evening, he saw a beautiful woman bathing. She was Bathsheba, the wife of Uriah, one of David's soldiers. David's lust got the better of him and he sent for her and slept with her that night. David probably thought no more of the incident until Bathsheba sent him word that she was pregnant. David feared a public scandal and so he worked out a plan to make it look as though it was Uriah's child. He arranged for him to be sent from the battle field as a messenger, and encouraged him to sleep with his wife that night before returning to his post the next day. But Uriah was a disciplined soldier who kept the rule that he should not have sex whilst on active service. So Uriah spent the night sleeping, with the king's slaves, at the palace gate. When David heard about this, he kept Uriah in Jerusalem for a further day and night, but even though David got him drunk, Uriah would not weaken. In desperation, David gave orders that Uriah should be put in the front line of the battle where he would most surely be killed. Once Uriah was out of the way, David married Bathsheba and she bore him a son.

Then Nathan, a prophet, came to the king and told him a story. It was of a rich man with large flocks and herds and of a poor man who had but one little lamb which was treated as the family pet. One day, the rich man needed to prepare a meal for a visitor but, being too mean to give one of his own animals, he took the poor man's lamb and served it up. David was furious when he heard this and swore to avenge this wrong. Then Nathan said to David, 'You are the man!' The Prophet's story was a parable about David and Uriah, and David had condemned himself. The incident about the lamb had not actually happened, but there is a sense in which this story is true, when it was put beside what David had actually done. The parable brought home to David his sin much more forcibly

A view of the old walled city of Jerusalem, now dominated by two large, domed mosques and with the high-rise buildings of modern Jerusalem in the background. David's city was smaller than the one there today within the walls which stretch across the middle of this picture, and it extended further to the left. From the time when David overcame its defences and made this his capital city, about 3,000 years ago, Jerusalem has been a symbol of Jewish patriotism.

than if the prophet had just charged in and condemned the king. David realised that he deserved to be punished and when the baby boy died, he accepted it as such. Later Bathsheba bore David another son, called Solomon, who became the next king.

Assignments

5 Which of the Ten Commandments did
  David break in this incident? (see page 38)
6 Explain how this parable was really a story
  about David. (You may wish to read it
  from the Bible with Nathan's explanation,
  in II Samuel ch. 12 vv. 1—14.)
7 Try to make up another parable which
  Nathan could havè used in the same
  situation.
8 Now that you have read about David, draw
  an emblem for him which you think is
  more suitable than the so-called 'Star of
  David' (e.g. a shepherd's crook).

At the end of Solomon's reign the kingdom
split into north and south, two independent
kingdoms. The southern kingdom of Judah,
with its stable, hereditary monarchy, survived
longer than the northern kingdom of Israel. It
was up to the prophets to make sense of the
situation when finally, even Judah and the
house of David were destroyed.

7 Prophecy

Prophets are a particular type of religious teacher. When we think of someone prophesying, we might think of him gazing into a crystal ball and predicting the future. But this is only half of the picture, and a distorted one at that. The word **prophet** comes from the Greek for 'one who proclaims something'. Prophets are men and women who feel compelled by God to deliver his message to others. They look around them and realise what will happen to people if they continue to behave in certain ways. They are not afraid to speak out about the *present* situation, and they are far-sighted enough to see where it will all lead in the *future*. So they *forth-tell* as well as *foretell*. If they think people are greedy and selfish, with everyone out for himself and having no real care for the needy, then they will warn of the disastrous outcome for society. They often see things which others are too short-sighted to see, or too afraid to think about. Their message is often harsh and unwelcome, and prophets are generally unpopular. Yet their work is necessary and springs from their love for God and for people and from a deep concern that things should be better.

Assignments

1 What is the difference between *forth*-telling and *fore*telling?
2 Many modern 'prophets' warn us to take more care of the natural world in which we live. 'If you let waste products from factories pollute our lakes and rivers *now*,' they say, 'there will be no fish in them *in the future*.'* Think of one other thing that you could criticise about the way we treat our world, and say what you think might be the future result of it.

There were many prophets in Israel at the time of the kings. Some of them were prophets because it was a popular profession and a means of making a living; and they probably followed in their fathers' footsteps. Others felt God's call to become prophets when they were already working at something else. Great individuals emerged from both of these categories. Their messages helped people to make sense of what was happening to them and were accepted as coming from God himself (although not always by the people at the time). When their words came true, they were remembered and recorded. They have been used by later readers as a guide and a warning, as they have tried to understand how God wants them to live.

Assignments

3 Notice the spellings of the following words, and the different meaning each has:
a **prophet** (the person who prophesies)
to **prophesy** (to preach God's message about the present situation and its future outcome)
a **prophecy** (the message preached by a prophet)
prophecy (the work of a prophet)
4 We have already come across some of the Old Testament prophets in this book.
a) Which prophet anointed David to be

king? (see page 45)

b) Which prophet rebuked David for his sins? (see page 49)

5 Many prophecies are introduced by the words 'Thus says the Lord', or something similar. The prophets claimed to be delivering God's message, although they had to interpret it and express it in human words. Read Amos ch. 3 and count how many times it refers to the words of the Lord.

6 a) Copy out Amos ch. 3 vv. 7—8.

b) Explain what these verses teach about prophecy.

Elijah

Elijah was an important prophet who lived in the northern kingdom of Israel about fifty years after the two kingdoms had separated. His name meant 'Yahweh is my God' and he was a great champion of God at a time when many Israelites were adopting the foreign, Canaanite religion.

King Ahab had married a Canaanite princess, called Jezebel, and she was doing all she could to promote her own religion. It was a fertility religion in which people made offerings to their 'Lord', Baal, and his sister-wife, Anat. Baal was said to be the son of the supreme

The Mother goddess (top) and Baal (right) — gods of the Canaanite nature religion, which the Israelite prophets condemned. Baal holds a club in his upraised hand and a spear in the other, the top of which may represent lightning, since he was the storm-god. Bulls' horns adorn his helmet because the bull stood for manliness and fertility. A library of clay tablets was found along with these carvings at Ras Shamra in Syria. They date from the fourteenth century BC and help scholars to understand the Canaanite religion better.

Mount Carmel, where Elijah won his contest with the prophets of Baal,
is now a built-up area in modern Israel.

God, El, whose wife was Asherah. Baal
worshippers tried to please these gods to
make sure that the orderly cycle of nature
would continue each year: that the dry and
wet seasons would follow each other regularly,
bringing the earth to life each time and
producing full harvests.

When the Israelites abandoned their nomadic
ways for a more settled life as farmers, they
were tempted to go over to this nature
religion. God had led them out of Egypt and
helped them fight their battles, but what
power did he have over the forces of nature?

It was this question that Elijah set himself
to answer. He presented a challenge to the
Israelites:

> 'How long will you sit on the fence? If the
> LORD [*i.e. Yahweh*] is God, follow him;
> but if Baal, then follow him.' (I Kings
> ch. 18 v. 21)

What follows is the most famous story about
Elijah. It tells of his lone contest with
hundreds of prophets of Baal on Mount
Carmel. He defied them to build an altar and
prepare a bull for sacrifice upon it, but to
leave it to Baal to send the fire. All day long
they called upon Baal, doing religious rituals
and working themselves up into frenzies.
Elijah taunted them:

> 'Call louder, for he is a god; it may be he
> is deep in thought, or engaged, or on a
> journey; or he may have gone to sleep and
> must be woken up.' (v. 27)

But Baal did not respond.

Then Elijah went to work. He took twelve
large stones, to represent each of the tribes of
Israel, and built an altar for God. He set his
bull-offering upon it and dug a trench round
it which was filled three times with four jars
of water (the number twelve again). Then he
called upon God:

> 'LORD God of Abraham, of Isaac, and of
> Israel, let it be known today that thou art
> God in Israel . . .' (v. 36)

Fire fell with such intense heat that even the
altar was burnt up. The people were convinced
of God's power over nature and, as a further
sign of his power, the prophets of Baal were
put to death.

7 a) Read the story in the Bible for
yourselves, from I Kings ch. 18
vv. 17—46.
   b) You could act out this story as a class;
or work out a dance sequence on it.
8 In those days, the cruel treatment of their
enemies was taken to show the strength of
the victors. Is this still so today, or might
we consider humane treatment of prisoners
to be a greater sign of strength?

There are two clear strands which are
woven together in the story of Elijah on
Mount Carmel. The first is set against the
background of a very long drought in Israel.
Elijah used this situation to show that it was
not Baal who sent or held back the rain, but
God. Elijah performed various rain-making
ceremonies: pouring out the precious water
to God on the altar, to symbolise his prayer
that God would drench the earth in rain.
Also, when he heard the rain coming, he
climbed to the top of Mount Carmel and
crouched to the ground, perhaps to symbolise
the rain-cloud which he sent his servant to
look for. On the seventh time he was sent, a
small cloud was spied on the horizon, and
soon the whole sky grew black with storm-
clouds and heavy rain began to fall.

The other strand in the story proved that it
was God who controlled the lightning, sending
fire from heaven; and not Baal, even though
he was considered to be the Storm-god.

Most prophets did not preach just about
things which we should recognise as 'religious',
they also spoke about politics, especially
foreign policies, and society in general. This
was because ancient societies were based on
religious beliefs. We have seen that the
Israelites regarded themselves as the people of
God and accepted the Ten Commandments as
the basis of their lives. These laws governed
how they should behave towards each other
as well as how they should worship God.

There are other important stories about
Elijah which show that his prophetic work

The storm-god (top) standing on a bull with
forked lightning in each hand. This engraving
(1½ metres high) comes from Assyria in the
eighth century BC.

This is part of a stained-glass window (right)
in Lincoln Cathedral, made in the nineteenth
century. It shows Elijah being taken up from
the earth. Read the story in II Kings ch. 2
vv. 7—18.

55

included 'religion', politics and social justice. You will see that the rest of the prophets in this book preach about these three things, although they may emphasise one thing more than another.

Assignments

  9 What were the three aspects of a prophet's message?
 10 Naboth's Vineyard is a famous story of Elijah as the champion of the poor and upholder of social justice. Your teacher may wish to study this story with you. It is in I Kings ch. 21.

The stories about Elijah were probably passed down among the prophets. They looked up to Elijah and emphasised his importance by adding personal and miraculous details, (the sort of thing that is found in the life-stories of great saints). Through such stories, we can see the impact that this great man had on the people of his day, particularly his followers. The most miraculous story about him is that he did not die, but was taken up to heaven by a whirlwind, in a fiery chariot, leaving the prophet Elisha to carry on his work.

This may have led to the idea that Elijah would return to earth some day. Right at the end of the Old Testament, we find this prophecy:

> Look, I will send you the prophet Elijah before the great and terrible day of the LORD comes. (Malachi ch. 4 v. 5)

The Jews still set aside a special chair for Elijah at their circumcision ceremonies, and set a place for him, with wine, at the Passover Supper. Most Jews do not really expect Elijah to take his seat, but it is a symbol that they still await the age of the Messiah, when God's faithful people will be rewarded.

8 Eighth-century prophets

Amos

About one hundred years after Elijah, there lived another great prophet, named Amos. One of the books in the Old Testament bears his name and records many of his prophecies. There is little in it directly about the man himself, for the prophetic books were more concerned to preserve 'the words of the Lord'. But we can try to build up a picture of him.

He was a countryman from the little town of Tekoa in the southern kingdom of Judah, a few miles south of the capital city, Jerusalem. He owned some sheep, but still needed to do seasonal work as a 'dresser of sycamore trees'. This involved puncturing the fig-like fruit to let the insects inside them escape. These fruit trees did not grow in the high, hilly area around Tekoa, so Amos had to travel away from home to find such work. We know that he also travelled as far north as Samaria, the capital of the northern kingdom of Israel. He probably went there to sell the produce from his sheep in the busy market-places.

Sheep grazing on a Judaean hillside where Amos was once a shepherd.

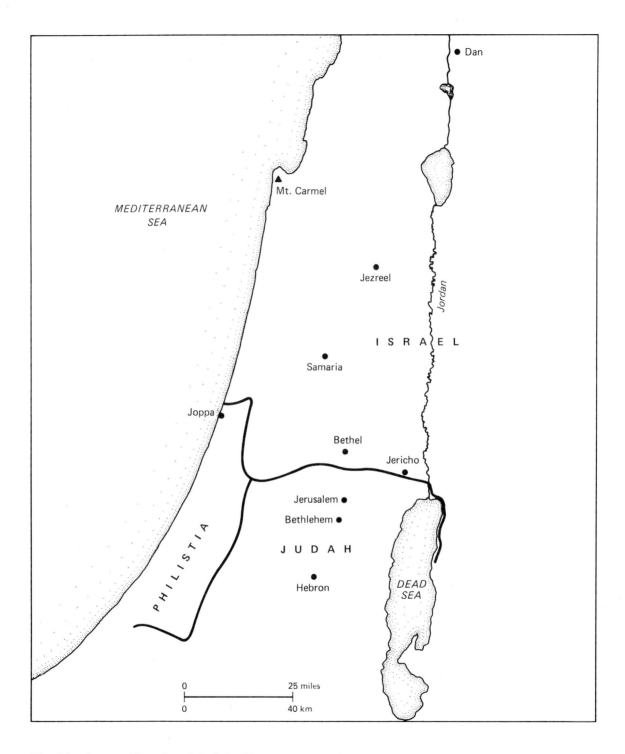

The kingdoms of Israel and Judah. The northern kingdom was the larger, extending from Dan to Bethel (both important religious centres) and with a fairly central capital city at Samaria. The southern kingdom kept the royal city of Jerusalem, the city of David, as its capital.

58

Amos lived during Israel's 'golden age'. Israel's enemies were too involved with each other to bother, for the time being, about this little country; and peace brought with it prosperity. Trade and industry prospered, and the rich merchants grew even richer. People seemed to think that this situation could go on for ever. The new class of rich people built themselves expensive houses, invested in second homes in the country, feasted on the best of food and generally lived a life of luxury.

Being a simple countryman, Amos was shocked by what he saw. He realised that some people were getting rich at the expense of others and that the gap between the rich and the poor was widening. He knew that such a divided society could not last for long.

Assignment

1 Look up Amos ch. 4 v. 1, ch. 5 vv. 10—12 and ch. 8 vv. 4—6, and describe the social injustices mentioned in them.

Amos was even more shocked when he realised that the rich people thought they were being religious. Amos knew that God was a God of justice. He knew that the Ten Commandments were not only about worshipping God faithfully but also about doing right by others. So he preached sternly to the Israelites in the name of God:

> I hate, I spurn your pilgrim-feasts;
>   I will not delight in your sacred
>   ceremonies.
> When you present your sacrifices and
>   offerings
>   I will not accept them,
> nor look on the buffaloes of your
>   shared-offerings.
> Spare me the sound of your songs;
> I cannot endure the music of your lutes.
> Let justice roll on like a river
> and righteousness like an ever-flowing
>   stream.
> (ch. 5 vv. 21—4)

The people knew that they were God's chosen ones, the people of the Covenant. They expected God to protect them and they thought the 'day of the Lord' was near, when God would set them up as the greatest nation on earth. Amos reminded them that the Covenant was a special agreement which promised punishment for deserting God's ways as well as rewards for following them. He told the people that God expected them to be much better than the surrounding nations who had never known God and that their own punishment would be much worse:

> Fools who long for the day of the LORD,
>   what will the day of the LORD mean to
>   you?
> It will be darkness, not light.
> (ch. 5 v. 18)

If you glance through the book of Amos, or indeed any of the books which record the prophets' words, you will notice that much of it is written in poetry. Hebrew poetry was not in verses, with lines ending in rhyming words; but it still had a rhythm, which comes across even in the English translation. Amos' prophecies were remembered easily because they rolled off the tongue and were full of powerful imagery. He spoke of God roaring (like a lion) from Jerusalem; he thought the remnant of Israel, after its destruction, would be of no more use than 'two shin bones or the tip of an ear' of a sheep that was killed by a lion; and he likened the rich women to cows. He had a vision of a man measuring a wall with a plumb-line to see if it was straight. Today, builders use spirit-levels to check that things are straight, and if they are not, they have to rebuild them. Amos used this symbol to teach that God expected Israel to measure up to his high expectations of them. Another vision produced the symbol of a basket of ripe summer fruit. Amos realised that Israel's end had come, and it was ripe for destruction. (There is a clever pun here in ch. 8 vv. 1—2 on the word *qais* (summer) and *qes* (end).)

It would not be far wrong to picture Amos walking about Samaria with bill-boards announcing 'Behold, the end is nigh!' No one likes to hear this sort of thing; and when

Amos had the cheek to preach against the king in the royal sanctuary of Bethel, he was warned by the priest-in-charge to go home. Whether he did or not, we do not know. What we do know is that his message of doom did eventually come true and his words of warning were remembered, too late.

Assignments

2 Look up the incident in Bethel, in Amos ch. 7 vv. 10–17. What do *you* think happened to Amos after this?
3 Amos was a countryman, arriving in a foreign city, and shocked by what he saw into prophesying against it. Imagine that you are in a similar situation today. You are a villager from one of the poor countries of the world, just arrived in a big city in the West. Is there anything that you would condemn? Write it in the form of a speech and prophesy where you think it will all lead.

Hosea

Hosea was another eighth-century prophet who lived at about the same time as Amos. He preached doom and destruction just as strongly, but realised that this was the only way that God would reform his people. Hosea, therefore, was a prophet of hope, because he saw beyond the punishment to a time when they would once more be worthy to be called God's people. Perhaps Hosea was able to see further than Amos because he was a northerner and it was his own country that he was condemning.

The book of Hosea is even more full of symbolism than that of Amos. It speaks of God as a surgeon who cuts open and then binds up the wound; just as it was necessary for God to hurt Israel in order to help it. Another time it likens God to a father who tenderly cared for his young son and taught

him to walk; just as God had guided Israel in its early days, when he led them out of Egypt, and was deeply hurt when they 'grew up' to reject him.

The symbol that is used again and again by Hosea is that of God as Israel's husband. The Exodus from Egypt was like the marriage between God and Israel, and the Covenant like the marriage contract. The Wilderness Period represented their honeymoon. When the people were unfaithful to God by worshipping Baal, this was seen as Israel committing adultery against her husband. Hosea preached that God would punish Israel with defeat at the hands of her enemies; just as a marriage might end in separation.

Sexual imagery like this could be found in the religion of Baalism which Hosea was condemning and which continued to tempt the Israelites. He boldly used this imagery of God's relationship with Israel to show that God, and not Baal, brought fertility to the crops and livestock, and that there was no need to worship any other gods.

Hosea was not the only prophet to use marriage imagery of God but, perhaps because of his own personal experiences, he took it furthest. It seems that Hosea also had an unfaithful wife. Yet he found that he still loved her and was prepared to take her back. He reasoned that, if human love can be this strong, God's loving-kindness must be greater still. Hosea believed that God would take back the Israelites after he had taught them a lesson, and would give them a fresh start as his chosen people.

Assignment

4 Read Hosea ch. 2 vv. 8—17, which is typical of the prophecies in the book of Hosea.
   a) What can we learn from vv. 8 and 13 about Baal worship?
   b) What symbol is used to describe the Baalim (plural of Baal) in vv. 12 and 13? (clue: 1_v_rs)
   c) In which verse do we find a sudden change of tune, as it swings from doom to hope?
   d) What symbol is used for God in v. 16?

The fall of the northern kingdom

Amos' and Hosea's prophecies of doom came true in 722 BC when the northern kingdom of Israel was destroyed by the Assyrians. The king and many of his subjects were taken to Assyria, and foreigners from the Assyrian empire were settled in Samaria instead. Any hope for the future Children of Israel now rested with the southern kingdom of Judah, which managed to survive for a further 136 years.

Isaiah

Another prophet at this time was First Isaiah. The book of Isaiah has 66 chapters, covering a period of at least two hundred years, which is far longer than the lifetime of one man. Scholars have divided the book into three parts, the divisions coming after chapters 39 and 55. It may be that the later parts were preached by followers of Isaiah.

The prophet of chapters 1—39 is known as First Isaiah, or Isaiah of Jerusalem. His task in the southern kingdom was much like that of Amos and Hosea in the north. He condemned similar social and religious evils and told the leaders of Judah that they were heading for disaster unless they changed their ways.

He gave symbolic names to two of his sons, to publicise his message. One was called *Shear-jashub*, which meant 'A remnant shall return'. There may have been some hope in this, but more likely it was a dreadful warning that most of the people would be destroyed. The other son was called *Maher-shalal-hash-baz*, which meant 'Speed-spoil-hasten-plunder', again warning that disaster would soon come, at the hands of their enemies.

Isaiah's message of doom can be seen in the parable he told about a vineyard. This story represents God's dealings with his chosen people. The owner of the vineyard symbolised God, and the vineyard was a symbol for the children of Israel. In this way, Isaiah warned that what happened to the vineyard would also happen to Judah.

Assignment

5 Read the Parable of the Vineyard in Isaiah ch. 5 vv. 1—7.
   a) Choose one word to describe how the owner had looked after his vineyard.
   b) Why did he eventually give up on it?
   c) Copy out v. 7.
   d) Draw a picture-strip to illustrate the different stages in this story of the vineyard.

A prophet—statesman

Isaiah of Jerusalem preached on and off over a long period, during which there were several political crises. Part of a prophet's job was to advise the kings; and Isaiah made full use of this. It was in Isaiah's time that Assyria destroyed the northern kingdom of Israel in 722, and brought the southern kingdom of Judah very near to a similar fate in 701. Israel and Judah were just two of several countries, including Syria and Egypt, which were trying to maintain their independence against the advancing might of Assyria. There were frequent alliances against Assyria, and Judah was drawn into these on more than one occasion.

In all these political crises, Isaiah's message was the same. He said that Judah should not trust in foreign nations or foreign gods, but they should put their trust in God alone, whose power extended over all nations:

> These are the words of the lord GOD the
> Holy One of Israel:
> Come back, keep peace, and you will be
> safe;
> in stillness, and in staying quiet, there
> lies your strength.
> (Isaiah ch. 30 v. 15)

During one such crisis, Isaiah used symbolic actions to bring home the force of his message. Although he was a respected figure at the royal court, for three years he went about Jerusalem dressed like a slave: naked and barefoot. Such would be the fate of the people of Judah if they trusted in Egypt to help them against Assyria!

Assignment

6 In this case Isaiah obviously agreed with the saying, 'Actions speak louder than words.' Can you think of some situations where a symbolic action is better than trying to express something in words? (e.g. clapping someone who has done well)

The call of Isaiah

It was a vision in the temple in Jerusalem which first led Isaiah to become a prophet. It is dated in the year of a king's death, and it could well have been at a specially grand ceremony for the enthronement of the next king; certainly the theme of kingship is very strong. As the building was filled with the heavy, scented smoke of burning incense, and perhaps resounding to the chanting of psalms, Isaiah gazed at the huge statues of winged creatures and imagined that he saw God enthroned there as the high and mighty King of Kings. He heard the heavenly creatures calling endlessly:

> Holy, holy, holy is the LORD of Hosts:
> the whole earth is full of his glory.
> (Isaiah ch. 6 v. 3b)

Isaiah was struck by this sense of God's holiness: that he is other than man, far above him, and in whose presence man is humbled. His reaction was to feel unworthy to set eyes upon God, and he was ashamed of his people who were not worshipping God with the single-minded devotion that God deserved. Then, in the vision, one of the heavenly creatures (a seraph) flew to Isaiah with a red-hot coal from the altar where the sacrifices were burned. He touched Isaiah's mouth with it to symbolise that Isaiah was being purified to speak the words of God. Only then did Isaiah have the courage to volunteer to do God's work as a prophet, a mouth-piece of God.

Assignments

7 Choose people to read the parts of the narrator, two seraphim and Isaiah. Let them read out loud Isaiah ch. 6 vv. 1—8, finishing with the words 'Here am I; send me.'

8 a) Why is fire a symbol for purification? Think of as many examples as possible from everyday life where fire is used to get rid of germs or rubbish.

Solomon's temple

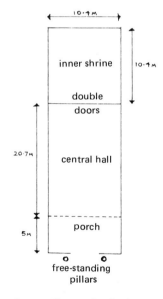

10·4 M

inner shrine | 10·4 M

double
doors

20·7 M | central hall

5 M | porch

free-standing
pillars

This plan shows the main features of the temple building: three chambers leading from one to the other, with the inner shrine, a perfect cube, in darkness at the far end.

No remains of Solomon's temple have ever been found. It was destroyed in 586 BC and the Second Temple was built on the same site. You can visit the Temple Mount in Jerusalem today, but it is not certain where the temple stood. The main building there today is the beautiful Muslim mosque, called the Dome of the Rock. It covers a massive rock which may have been the altar of Solomon's temple, or perhaps it was the platform on which the inner shrine of the temple was built.

There have been many attempts to draw or make scale models of Solomon's temple following the detailed description given in I Kings ch. 6, although this description may have been influenced by knowledge of the later temple. Solomon's temple was relatively small: we should do better to think of it as a royal chapel than as a cathedral. It was built to house the Ark of the Covenant in the inner shrine, known as the 'holy of holies'. The people would have gathered outside, where the altar for animal sacrifices stood.

A cherub(?) carved in ivory, from ninth-century Samaria, the capital city of Israel.

b) Can you think of another, perhaps better, symbol of purification?
9 a) Look up the description of the cherubim in the temple, in I Kings ch. 6 vv. 23—8. The cherubim and seraphim may have been the same: imaginary, heavenly creatures, half-human and half-animal. (The singular of cherubim is a cherub and of seraphim is a seraph.)
b) Do you know of any other imaginary human—animal creatures?

Isaiah (left) painted on a pillar in a church in Rome by the famous Italian artist, Raphael, in 1512. The cherubim in the background show how they were imagined in the artist's day.

The Messiah

Isaiah's message, like that of Amos and Hosea, was chiefly one of doom. Yet there are also some hopeful prophecies, although some scholars think these were added later, after the Exile, and were not preached by First Isaiah at all.

Some of the hopeful prophecies are about the Messiah (later, in Greek, called the Christ). He was to be the saviour, sent by God to his chosen people. He would set up God's kingdom on earth, and rule in justice and righteousness from Jerusalem.

The word Messiah was another term for 'king'. The actual word means 'anointed one' for their kings were not crowned but anointed with holy oil. At first, the Messiah was expected to be another great king like David (the 'Son of David'). The Davidic kings ruled from Jerusalem for about four hundred years, and as each new prince was born and each new king enthroned, everyone must have wondered if this was the Messiah they had been waiting for. The following passage echoes this:

> For a boy has been born for us, a son given to us
>> to bear the symbol of dominion on his shoulder;
>> and he shall be called
>> in purpose wonderful, in battle God-like,
>> Father for all time, Prince of peace.
> Great shall the dominion be,
>> and boundless the peace
> bestowed on David's throne and on his kingdom,
> to establish it and sustain it
>> with justice and righteousness
>> from now and for evermore.
> The zeal of the LORD of Hosts shall do this.
> (Isaiah ch. 9 vv. 6—7)

King followed king, failing even to live up to the original David. Eventually this hope for the Messiah was thrown into the distant future. Judah, the present kingdom of David, might be destroyed, but one day, it was thought, God would send them a New David. Another passage in Isaiah expresses this idea, for it speaks of the Messiah coming from the roots of Jesse. Jesse had been the father of David, so we see here the idea that God would start all over again and fulfil his promises to his chosen people in a completely New Age:

> Then a shoot shall grow from the stock
>   of Jesse,
> and a branch shall spring from his roots.
> The spirit of the LORD shall rest upon
>   him, a spirit of wisdom and
>   understanding, a spirit of counsel and
>   power, a spirit of knowledge and the
>   fear of the LORD.
> (Isaiah ch. 11 vv. 1—2)

A fellow-prophet, Micah, had a similar idea. He prophesied that the Messiah would come from Bethlehem, the birth-place of David. Once again, we see the idea of a new beginning.

Assignments

10 Why did the people hope for a Messiah?
11 Copy out Micah ch. 5 v. 2.
12 The British monarch is anointed by the Archbishop of Canterbury as well as being crowned.
   a) What other symbols are given to the king or queen at the coronation?
   b) Try to discover the symbolic significance of these symbols. (Look them up in an encyclopaedia.)

The British Crown Jewels, used at the Coronation Service.

9 Prophets of the Exile

Jeremiah

About one hundred years after Isaiah, there lived another great prophet, named Jeremiah. He also preached doom and destruction in Jerusalem, because the people were still worshipping idols and refusing to live in God's way. They had learnt nothing from the fall of the northern state of Israel, nor from the preaching of Isaiah. Jeremiah realised that they were too far gone to change themselves now:

> Can the Nubian change his skin,
>   or the leopard its spots?
> And you? Can you do good,
>   you who are schooled in evil?
> Therefore I will scatter you like chaff
>   driven by the desert wind.
> (Jeremiah ch. 13 vv. 23—4)

Assignments

1 'A leopard can't change its spots' has become a proverb. What does it mean?
2 a) Read Jeremiah ch. 19 vv. 1—5 and 10—11.

b) What symbolic action does Jeremiah use to illustrate his message on this occasion?

Jeremiah was a very sensitive person who suffered a great deal because of his message. He became a prophet when still a young man, and gave up any thought of marriage and children so that he could devote himself to his work. His family and friends were embarrassed by him and his own townspeople made fun of him. On one occasion at the temple he was given a beating and put in the stocks by the priest-in-charge; and another time he was set upon by everyone there. At best, he was regarded as a public nuisance and at worst, a traitor. Jeremiah was often depressed and he cried out to God in despair; but deep down he knew that he had to go on and that God would stand by him, even if everyone else turned against him.

Assignments

3 Read Jeremiah ch. 20 vv. 14—18 and explain how Jeremiah was feeling when he composed this.
4 Read Jeremiah ch. 15 vv. 16—18 and put into your own words the complaint he is making here to God.
5 What does it tell us about Jeremiah's relationship with God, that he was able to speak so freely to him?
6 Can you think of a modern example of someone who, like Jeremiah, has suffered for standing up for what he or she believed to be true?

The temple sermon

Jeremiah believed that the people were blind to the truth about themselves because of their false trust in the temple. They thought that God would never desert his own temple and therefore, as long as the temple stood, God was with them and they were safe, and nothing else mattered. So the temple had become a sort of lucky mascot and their religion had become a superstition.

Jeremiah had the nerve to preach within the temple itself that God would destroy even his temple if need be:

> You keep saying, 'This place is the temple of the LORD, the temple of the LORD, the temple of the LORD!' This catchword of yours is a lie; put no trust in it. Mend your ways and your doings, deal fairly with one another, do not oppress the alien, the orphan, and the widow, shed no innocent blood in this place, do not run after other gods to your own ruin. Then will I let you live in this place, in the land which I gave long ago to your forefathers for all time. You gain nothing by putting your trust in this lie. (Jeremiah ch. 7 vv. 4—8)

This sermon led to an uproar in the temple and Jeremiah was nearly lynched. The royal officers restored order and Jeremiah was released. Presumably after this incident, Jeremiah was forbidden to preach in the temple again. Not to be put off, he dictated a sermon to his secretary and sent *him* to read it in the temple at an important gathering. Word eventually reached the king about this, who personally destroyed the scroll on which Jeremiah's words were written.

Assignments

7 In the passage quoted, Jeremiah said the temple could not save the Jews. What did he say *could* save them?

8 a) List or draw a few things that people have as lucky charms and mascots.
   b) Do you have any lucky mascots? (e.g. do you take anything special into examinations with you to bring you luck?) How much faith do you put in them?
   c) Why is it superstitious to regard something as lucky or unlucky?

9 a) If you were Jeremiah, what would you do now that the king himself has destroyed your scroll and you are forbidden to preach in the temple?
   b) Look up Jeremiah ch. 36 vv. 27—32 to find out what Jeremiah did, and make a brief note of it.

Judah had no reason to be so confident, for it was a time of extreme political danger. The threat of Assyria eventually gave way to the even greater threat of Babylon. The big powers of Assyria and Egypt were defeated by Babylon, and Jeremiah saw that it was madness for a little country like Judah to try to resist. But resist they did, and Babylon laid siege to Jerusalem in 597. The king of Judah soon gave in and the royalty, the leading men of the city, the soldiers and the important craftsmen were all taken off into exile in Babylon.

Jeremiah continued to say that they should accept Babylonian rule. He illustrated this by wearing a farm-animal's yoke across his shoulders. He believed that God controlled all nations and had given the Jews into the hands of the Babylonians. But many Jews still lived in hope. They thought that the first exiles would soon return and that Judah could become independent once more. Jeremiah warned them that a rebellion would lead to the destruction of Jerusalem. He was regarded as a traitor and kept under house-arrest.

Judah did rebel and King Nebuchadnezzar of Babylon came with his army and surrounded Jerusalem. The siege dragged on until the people in Jerusalem were desperate. The king of Judah tried to escape by night but was captured. The city walls were knocked down and Jerusalem, including the temple, was burnt to the ground. In 586 another long line of exiles were taken off to

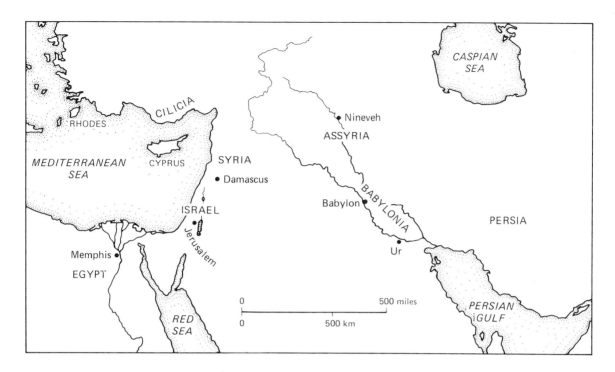

Map showing Israel surrounded by its enemies: first Egypt; then Syria; then Assyria which destroyed the northern kingdom of Israel; then Babylon which destroyed the southern kingdom of Judah.

Babylon. Jeremiah himself was allowed to stay.

Assignments

10 a) What is the purpose of a yoke?
    b) Was it a good symbol to represent Jeremiah's message that Judah must be brought under Babylon's control?
11 Paint an abstract picture of the destruction of Jerusalem.
12 The feelings of the Jews as they went into exile are expressed very strongly in Psalm 137. Read this Psalm and, if possible, listen to it set to music (e.g. from the musical, *Godspell*).

The new covenant

Jeremiah had made no bones about the disaster that was coming, and yet he also saw beyond it a ray of hope. Even in the last days of Jerusalem, he had taken the opportunity to buy up a piece of land that was in the family. This was done as a sign that he believed the exiles would eventually return and rebuild their lives in Judah.

Jeremiah believed that God could make a fresh start after the destruction. He described this as a new covenant. He thought that, once the temple lay in ruins, people could come to know God much more personally (as Jeremiah himself did). The kingdoms of Israel and Judah had been destroyed because they were corrupt nations, and the innocent had suffered with the guilty; but Jeremiah looked forward to a time when each individual would be answerable to God for himself.

Assignments

13 a) Copy out the symbolic saying in Jeremiah ch. 31 v. 29.

b) Explain what it means in connection with what is said above about personal or collective guilt.

14 Read the passage on the new covenant in Jeremiah ch. 31 vv. 31—4.

Ezekiel

Ezekiel is the last of the Major Prophets (Isaiah, Jeremiah and Ezekiel), that is, those who have very long books in the Old Testament.

The book of Ezekiel tells us that he was deported to Babylon with the first exiles of 597. He seems to have been a rather strange person who saw fantastic visions and had experiences of being beside himself with emotion so that, on occasions, he was unable to speak or move. All of these religious experiences had symbolic meanings for him as a prophet.

His call to become a prophet came in a vision of God's splendour which overwhelmed him. He saw this amazing vision in the middle of 'a storm wind . . . a vast cloud with flashes of fire and brilliant light about it' and he heard a sound 'like the noise of a great torrent or of a cloud-burst'. The vision was framed in an arch of light above it, which he described as 'like a rainbow in the clouds on a rainy day' (Ezekiel ch. 1 vv. 4, 24 and 28). He heard a voice commanding him to preach to his own people, although he was warned that they would not listen to him. In the vision he was told to eat a scroll of the words of doom which he must preach:

> Then I saw a hand stretched out to me, holding a scroll. He unrolled it before me, and it was written all over on both sides with dirges and laments and words of woe. Then he said to me, 'Man, eat what is in front of you, eat this scroll; then go and speak to the Israelites.' So I opened my mouth and he gave me the scroll to eat. Then he said, 'Man, swallow this scroll I give you, and fill yourself full.' So

I ate it, and it tasted as sweet as honey. (Ezekiel ch. 2 v. 9—ch. 3 v. 3)

For seven days after this vision Ezekiel lived in a daze, and then he set about his prophetic work.

Assignments

15 a) How do you usually feel and react when there is a storm?
   b) Describe, or paint a picture of, the most violent storm you have ever witnessed.

16 Ezekiel's vision was such a strange experience that he found it difficult to describe in ordinary language. So he used symbolic language. You will see this by the number of times he says that something was *like* something else. Read Ezekiel ch. 1 vv. 4—28, counting the number of times 'like', 'as if' or 'as it were' occur.

17 Jeremiah also described the words he had to preach as something he felt in his body which he could not hold in. Look up Jeremiah ch. 20 v. 9 and copy out what it says the word of the Lord was like for him.

It is not clear whether Ezekiel returned to Jerusalem to carry out his prophetic work, or whether he preached in Babylon, hoping that his message would reach those back home by letters and travellers. His early message was one of doom and judgement, until the final blow came in 586 and Jerusalem was destroyed. The prophets had been right in realising that it was necessary for both the Israelite kingdoms to fall, before the people would come to their senses and listen to the word of God. But now that the worst had happened, Ezekiel could change his tune. He knew that if the all-powerful God could bring his people to their knees, he could also raise them up once more. Out of death and despair could come life and hope. He began to rally the dispirited survivors by preaching that

The Vision of Ezekiel, painted by Raphael in 1518. In Raphael's day, artists were influenced by Greek and Roman art, so that God here looks more like Zeus (see page 89) than the Hebrew idea of God. The four winged creatures are also a rather free interpretation of Ezekiel's vision and portray the man, lion, ox and eagle which the Church used to symbolise the four Evangelists: Matthew, Mark, Luke and John. Try to paint your own picture of this vision, closer to the prophet's own description of it in Ezekiel ch. 1 (notice especially vv. 5—11 and 26—7). Can you see any similarities between the painting here and another one by Raphael on page 64?

God would make a new beginning for his people.

This new hope is illustrated most vividly in Ezekiel's vision of the valley of dry bones:

> The hand of the LORD came upon me, and he carried me out by his spirit and put me down in a plain full of bones. He made me go to and fro across them until I had been round them all; they covered the plain, countless numbers of them, and they were very dry. . . . I began to prophesy as he had bidden me, and as I prophesied there was a rustling sound and the bones fitted themselves together. As I looked, sinews appeared upon them, flesh covered them, and they were overlaid with skin, but there was no breath in them. Then he said to me, 'Prophesy to the wind, prophesy, man, and say to it, These are the words of the Lord GOD: Come, O wind, come from every quarter and breathe into these slain, that they may come to life.' I began to prophesy as he had bidden me: breath came into them; they came to life and rose to their feet, a mighty host. He said to me, 'Man, these bones are the whole people of Israel.' (Ezekiel ch. 37 vv. 1—2 and 7—10)

So the bones represented Israel and Judah, in ruins, but able to be built up again by the power of God.

Assignments

18 Perhaps your class could learn the Negro spiritual about the valley of dry bones.
19 Ezekiel's vision symbolises resurrection to new life. Another symbol for this is the change from winter to spring: all looks bleak and dead until the bulbs push their way up through the soil, buds appear and the leaves clothe the bare trees once more. Spring makes us aware that everything around us is bursting into life. Can you think of any other symbols which represent this change from death to life? (The drawings may give you some ideas.)
20 Work out a dance sequence on the theme of 'New Life'.

Ezekiel was from a priestly family and his hopes for the future centred upon a restored temple in Jerusalem. He envisaged a holy nation that would be guided by the priests and by the religious laws. The last nine chapters of the book of Ezekiel record in great detail his vision of the restoration: of the temple, the holy city and the land of Israel. He saw God enthroned once more in his holy temple. He saw life-giving waters flowing out from the temple and growing into a big river which watered the desert areas. This was a symbol that the temple would be the source of the nation's life.

In this way, prophetic authority was given for the eventual rebuilding of the temple as the heart of the new Jewish community, and for the importance of the priesthood after the Exile. The prophet's hopes for the New Israel are expressed in this further passage, where he foresees the exiles returned, having turned their backs upon their old sins, and living in a new relationship with God:

An egg, chrysalis and phoenix.

Life-giving water.

Say therefore, these are the words of the Lord GOD: I will gather them from among the nations and assemble them from the countries over which I have scattered them, and I will give them the soil of Israel. When they come into it, they will do away with all their vile and abominable practices. I will give them a different heart and put a new spirit into them; I will take the heart of stone out of their bodies and give them a heart of flesh. Then they will conform to my statutes and keep my laws. They will become my people, and I will become their God. (Ezekiel ch. 11 vv. 17—20)

Assignments

21 Draw a picture of Ezekiel's symbol of the river of life flowing out from the temple. (You may wish to read the description first in Ezekiel ch. 47 vv. 1—12.)

22 a) Why is water a symbol of life?
   b) Write a short story to emphasise the importance of water.

23 What does it mean if someone is said to have a 'heart of stone', as in the passage above? What does it mean to say that someone has a heart of gold, or is warm-hearted, or is cold-hearted? Can you think of any other similar sayings?

Conclusion

The destruction of the kingdoms of Israel and Judah might have been the end of the story. It would have been easy for the survivors to have given up their religion altogether and to have worshipped the gods of the Babylonians, amongst whom they now lived. If it had not been for their prophets, they would have assumed that the gods of the victors were the best.

Amos, Hosea, First Isaiah, Jeremiah, Ezekiel and others had warned them that they were heading for disaster, and that it would be their own fault. The prophets had come to realise that God rules supreme and that he would make use of the surrounding nations to punish his own rebellious people. So the fall of Jerusalem, like the fall of the northern kingdom many years before, was accepted as a sign of God's strength and justice, and not of his weakness. The prophets had also sown seeds of hope for the future, so that the people did not give up.

1 Which of these prophets does *not* have a book in the Bible named after him?

ELIJAH — AMOS — HOSEA — ISAIAH

— JEREMIAH — EZEKIEL

2 Using the list in No. 1 again, which are known as the Major Prophets?

3 The prophets were concerned with worship, politics and social justice, but each emphasised a particular aspect. Copy out the diagram below and join each prophet to his most important concern, as I have done with Elijah. You must be prepared to justify your answer.

4 Which of these prophets preached in the northern kingdom, and which in the southern kingdom? Copy out the list below and draw a line where the division comes, writing 'Israel' in one part and 'Judah' in the other, where appropriate.

ELIJAH
AMOS
HOSEA
ISAIAH
JEREMIAH
EZEKIEL

WORSHIP ————————————→ Elijah

                                        Amos

POLITICS

                                        Hosea

SOCIAL JUSTICE

                                        Isaiah

10 Widening their horizons

Parables

The two stories in this chapter are both parables. We have already had some examples of parables in this book: Nathan's story to David about the poor man's lamb (see page 49) and Isaiah's Parable of the Vineyard (see page 61). You will have gathered that parables are stories with a lesson to teach. They are made up, but are about everyday life and could well have happened. (Do you remember that David thought there really was a rich man who had killed the lamb?) The word **parable** means 'to put beside' because a parable is not just an interesting story, but one with a meaning running alongside it. So parables are symbolic stories: they are not just what they appear to be, but they stand for something else.

The Exile and Restoration

The stories of Ruth and Jonah were written after the Exile, when the remnant of the Jews had begun to rebuild their lives in and around Jerusalem. During their exile in Babylon, they had kept very much to themselves so that they could encourage each other in their religion and not be tempted to adopt foreign beliefs. The priests among them kept a record of the rules about their religion and about temple-worship, even though they no longer had a temple. They encouraged the people to keep strictly to these religious laws, like observing the Sabbath as a day of rest and circumcising their baby boys. Not only did such things mark them out from the Babylonians, but they were constant reminders to the Jews that they still lived under God's laws because he was still present with them. Their history books also became very important because they formed a link with their past. So they still had a sense of belonging to the People of God even though they now had no holy land, no Davidic king and no temple.

In this way, Judaism survived. Some Jews prospered in Babylon and settled there; but others kept alive in their children the desire to return to Jerusalem. Their wishes came true when, about fifty years later, Babylon was defeated by Cyrus of Persia and the Jews were free to return. Over the years that followed, small groups of Jews undertook the hazardous journey.

At first the new settlers in Jerusalem had a miserable time of it, until they were organised by two great Jews: Nehemiah and Ezra. Nehemiah was sent from the Persian court to supervise the rebuilding of the city walls. This was very important, for it meant that the inhabitants could defend themselves from attack. We are told that Nehemiah became the governor of Judah and established law and order there.

Ezra was also sent by the king of Persia. As a priest, he could put in order the religious affairs of Judah. Although the people had built the Second Temple, their religion had become very slack. Many of them were married to foreign wives which meant that their children were not being brought up as Jews. Many religious laws and festivals, including the Sabbath, were not being observed properly. Many priests and Levites (the servers in the temple after the

The walls of Jerusalem, built for defence.

Exile) were corrupt, and the priesthood generally lacked authority.

Ezra brought a law-book to Judah and imposed its laws very strictly. We do not know for sure which book it was, but it may well have been the Pentateuch since this was edited at about this time. At a great ceremony, all the people gathered to confess their sins and they agreed to live by the religious laws.

Assignments

1 Look up the *History Chart* on page 7.
   a) When did Ezra and Nehemiah go to Jerusalem?
   b) How long was this after the exiles were first allowed to return?
2 Read Ezra ch. 9 vv. 1—6.
   a) What sin had many of the Jews committed?
   b) What actions symbolised Ezra's shame and sorrow on behalf of the people?
   c) In what circumstances today might someone say 'I'm tearing my hair out'?
3 Read Ezra ch. 10 vv. 1—4. What did the people agree to do about their sin?

Ruth

It was against this background that the book of Ruth was written, even though the story is set in the time of the judges. Whether or not Ruth actually lived, we do not know, but the story of Ruth served as a parable, with a message for the Jews of the Restoration. The idea of the story may even have been sparked off by Ezra's reforms in which the Jews divorced their foreign wives. For Ruth was a foreigner, and yet she is portrayed as a good woman and a faithful worshipper of God. What is more, she is said to be the great-grandmother of no less a person than David himself. So the story shows that even the greatest king of the Jews had foreign blood in him.

The message of the parable is clear: just as Ruth was welcomed by the Hebrews and became a respected member of their community, so should foreigners still be welcome to join the People of God. The Jews had become too inward-looking after the Exile and so concerned with their own holiness that they feared any contact with Gentiles (non-Jews). Now the other side of the argument is being put: that God welcomes anyone who will serve him faithfully; and the Jews should be glad to tell others about their God and their religion.

The book of Ruth is only four chapters long and full of human interest. You should read it in the Bible for yourselves. It begins with a Hebrew family moving to the neigh-bouring country of Moab when food was in short supply at home. The family consisted of Naomi, her husband and their two sons. They settled in Moab and, after her husband died,

The Story of Ruth (right and page 78) by Thomas Matthews Rooke, painted around 1876. He has shown the three events which he considered most important. If he had instead painted four scenes, what would you expect the missing picture to show?

Ruth and Naomi (right) return as widows to Bethlehem.

(left): Boaz meets Ruth as she gathers some left-over corn in his fields.

(right): Naomi nurses the son of Ruth and Boaz.

her sons married Moabite girls, called Orpah and Ruth. When tragedy struck again, and both men died, Naomi decided that she had no reason to stay in Moab. When she returned to her home-town of Bethlehem, Orpah stayed behind in Moab but Ruth would not desert her mother-in-law.

The two widows settled in Bethlehem and had to rely on charity in order to live. The law made some provision for people like them:

When you reap the harvest of your land, you shall not reap right into the edges of your field; neither shall you glean the loose ears of your crop; you shall not completely strip your vineyard nor glean the fallen grapes. You shall leave them for the poor and the alien. I am the LORD your God. (Leviticus ch. 19 vv. 9—10)

Ruth caught the eye of Boaz, the rich, elderly owner of the fields where she gathered the bits of corn that were left over. He made sure she was well looked after and treated respectfully by his workmen.

Naomi was delighted when she heard about

this, especially as Boaz was a close relative of hers and the law made it his duty to keep her family-line going now that her two sons had died without children. So Naomi began match-making. The incident of how she persuaded Ruth to seduce Boaz when he was drunk is described quite discreetly in chapter 3. Boaz was flattered by the attentions of this young woman and he decided to marry her. We are held in suspense while a closer relative, who had first claim on Ruth, is dealt with. Finally Ruth and Boaz got married and Ruth bore him a son who became the grandfather of King David.

Assignments

4 The names in this story may have been long remembered because of their connection with David, or they may have been invented for their symbolic meanings:
   a) Which of the girls' names do you think meant 'companion' and which meant 'turning away'?
   b) Naomi's sons had names which meant 'sickness' and 'pining away'. What sense can you make of this within the story?
   c) Look up Ruth ch. 1 vv. 20—1 to find out the meaning of Mara, the name Naomi ('pleasantness') wanted to be called in her sorrow.
   d) Boaz meant 'in him is strength'. To whom do you think 'him' refers?
5 Copy out Ruth's words in Ruth ch. 1 v. 16.
6 In Ruth ch. 4 we discover, in passing, quite a lot about legal matters in Israel.
   a) Where did legal hearings take place? (v. 1)
   b) How many witnesses were needed? (v. 2)
   c) What was the sign that an agreement had been made to buy the plot of land? (vv. 7—8)
7 Read Ruth ch. 4 vv. 13—22.
   a) Make a list of the names from Boaz to David.
   b) Why was it so important for Naomi to have a grandchild? (v. 14)

Jonah

The book of Jonah is included in the list of the 12 Minor Prophets although it is very different from the rest of them. Unlike the others, it is not a collection of prophecies, but is the story of one incident in the life of the prophet called Jonah. It is set in the eighth century BC but was written by an anonymous author several hundred years later. It is lacking in historical details about the eighth century, and describes Nineveh in such a legendary way that it must have been written a long time after the destruction of that great city in 621 BC. Also, like the book of Ruth, its message makes most sense after the Exile, when the Jews had become totally concerned with rebuilding their own lives.

The story tells how Jonah was called by God to preach to Nineveh, the capital city of Assyria (see map on page 69). Jonah did not want to do this, for the Assyrians had been the hated enemies of the Israelites and in the eighth century they had destroyed the northern kingdom of Israel and brought the southern kingdom to its knees. Jonah tried in vain to avoid the mission that God called him to do. He escaped on a ship bound for Tarshish in the western Mediterranean, the opposite direction to Assyria. We are told that God let loose a hurricane and the ship was in danger of sinking. When all other measures had failed, the sailors realised that it was Jonah's fault, and the storm only calmed down when they had thrown him overboard. God had Jonah swallowed up by 'a great fish' (there is no mention of a whale) and after three days and nights he was vomited out onto dry land.

Again Jonah was ordered to go to Nineveh and this time he obeyed, preaching: 'In forty days Nineveh shall be overthrown!' The people of Nineveh repented when they heard this message of doom and they decided to give up their wicked ways. They dressed in rough sackcloth and went without food and drink to punish themselves and show God how sorry they were. When God saw this, he

forgave them and did not destroy them after all.

Jonah was angry that his prophecy had not come true and he wished he were dead. As he sat and sulked, God caused a plant to grow up by him to give him shade. Jonah was grateful for it. But the next day, God made the plant die and, as the sun beat down on him, Jonah found himself once more in the depths of despair. The story ends abruptly with God rebuking Jonah for being sad about a solitary plant that he had neither planted nor tended, when he could not accept God's mercy on the city of Nineveh with its many inhabitants.

'Then the LORD spoke to the fish and it spewed Jonah out on to the dry land.' (Jonah ch. 2 v.10)

A castor-oil plant, such as grew up over Jonah's head to give him shade.

Assignments

8 Act out the scene described in Jonah ch. 1.

9 What did dressing in sackcloth symbolise?

10 What do we say people are doing when they deliberately go without food and drink for a time?

11 Try to find and cut out some pictures from magazines which express the feelings of Jonah in ch. 4, or draw a series of pictures of your own to illustrate them.

It is pointless to ask if it is possible to survive in a whale's stomach, for this is a parable, a symbolic story. It uses this folk-tale theme to add colour to the story and to bring Jonah quickly back to land. The purpose of the story is not to record a historical incident, but to teach the truth of God's love for everyone and not just the Jews. The name **Jonah** means 'dove', which was used as an image for Israel. The figure of

Jonah in this story could well represent Israel, which was swallowed up in the Exile but saved from extinction by God for a purpose. Yet their deliverance had left the Jews more arrogant and narrow-minded as the 'chosen people'.

Assignments

12 Look up Jonah ch. 1 v. 16 and ch. 3 v. 5. Which foreigners were brought to belief in God?

13 How are the symbols of 'doves' and 'hawks' used in descriptions of wars today?

14 Can you think of a modern fairy-tale which has its two principal characters swallowed by a big fish?

Conclusion

Both Ruth and Jonah taught a similar lesson: that the Jews should widen their horizons; they should be more out-going and more compassionate to the rest of the world. While many Jews after the Exile were rebuilding their own lives around their religion, busy saving themselves, others realised that God had chosen them for a much bigger purpose. They thought the Jews were part of God's plan to save the whole world. Therefore, they should look beyond themselves, setting an example to others and teaching them God's ways.

One prophet of the Exile who is remembered particularly for this attitude was Second Isaiah. The chapters he is thought to have spoken (Isaiah ch. 40—55) include the so-called *Servant Songs*. There are different opinions as to who the 'suffering servant' was meant to be (some think it refers to the prophet who is speaking, or to the future Messiah). One passage says that the servant was Israel i.e. not one person at all, but a symbol for the whole of Israel. It could be referring particularly to the faithful remnant amongst the Israelites who suffered innocently because of the sins of the whole nation. This is the passage:

He said to me, 'You are my servant,
  Israel through whom I shall win glory';
(Isaiah ch. 49 v. 3a)

It continues:

I will make you a light to the nations,
to be my salvation to earth's farthest
  bounds.
(v. 6b)

This seems to be saying that the Jews were called by God to serve others and to enlighten them with the knowledge of God.

Assignment

15 Explain what the books of Ruth and Jonah were trying to teach the Jews about their attitudes to non-Jews.

Jonah ch. 2 is a psalm (a religious song). It may have been composed before the book of Jonah was written, and added because it was so appropriate. Here are some parts of it:

Thou didst cast me into the depths, far out
    at sea,
        and the flood closed round me;
all thy waves, all thy billows, passed over
    me.

The water about me rose up to my neck;
    the ocean was closing over me.
Weeds twined above my head
    in the troughs of the mountains;
    I was sinking into a world
whose bars would hold me fast for ever.
But thou didst bring me up alive from the
    pit, O LORD my God.
(vv. 3, 5—6)

A similar passage from Psalm 69:

    Save me, O God;
for the waters have risen up to my neck.

I sink in muddy depths and have no foot-
    hold;
I am swept into deep water, and the flood
    carries me away.
I am wearied with crying out, my throat is
    sore,
my eyes grow dim as I wait for God to help
    me.
(vv. 1—3)

1 The sea is a source of terror to many people. If you have ever thought you were drowning, you would know why. It is quite common to sink under the water when learning to swim, and even a matter of seconds can seem like ages. If you have ever felt fear in connection with water, describe or write a poem about your experience.
2 Why do you think so many people call upon God when they are in danger?
3 a) Why are people fascinated by stories of survival, as in the 'disaster movie' *Towering Inferno?*
   b) Can you think of any other films on a similar theme?

dīm9: ut uetera destruam9. Et tamē tū
diligētissime legerit. sciat magis nīa
scripta intelligi: que nō in terciū uas
trāssusa coacuerit: sed statim de prelo
purissime ōmēdata teste: suū saprē ser-
uauerit. Incipiut parabole salomōis

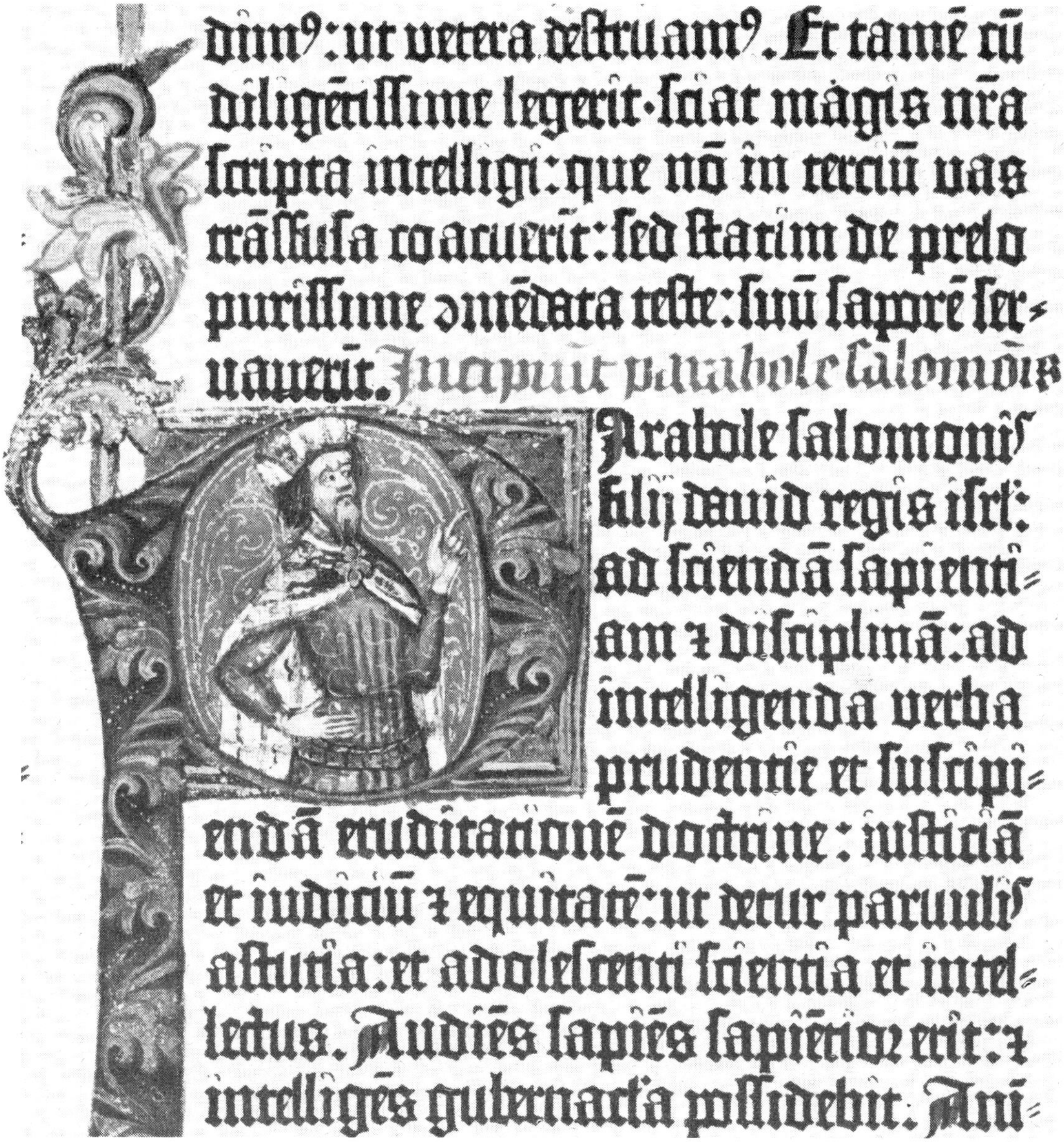

Prabole salomonis
filij dauid regis isrł:
ad sciendā sapienti-
am ꝛ disciplinā: ad
intelligenda uerba
prudentie et suscipi-
endā eruditationē doctrine: iusticiā
et iudiciū ꝛ equitatē: ut detur paruulis
astutia: et adolescenti scientia et intel-
lectus. Audiēs sapiēs sapiētior erit: ꝛ
intelligēs gubernacla possidebit. Ani-

The wisdom referred to in this chapter is not so much to do with passing examinations as with common sense about life in general. People in every age reflect upon life: thinking about its sorrows and its joys, asking about the meaning of it all and how best to behave. This leads to wise sayings, or **proverbs**, which are passed down from one generation to another. Some people think more deeply about these things and teach or write down their ideas. Today we call them **philosophers**, meaning 'lovers of wisdom', but in biblical times they were the scribes. The scribes were educated in reading and writing, and passed on the wisdom of their age.

The People of God tried to make sense of life within the framework of their belief in the one, good God who was the source of all wisdom. One of their proverbs says:

> The first step to wisdom is the fear of the LORD,
> and knowledge of the Holy One is understanding . . .
> (Proverbs ch. 9 v. 10)

Many of their wise sayings, therefore, are religious. The Wisdom of Israel was written up after the Exile in books like Proverbs, Job and Ecclesiastes, but much of it came from earlier times. King Solomon, in particular, had a reputation for wisdom, so much so that all the sayings in the book of Proverbs are said to have come from him.

Assignments

1 Write down a popular proverb and explain in your own words what it teaches.
2 *Do not withhold discipline from a boy; take the stick to him, and save him from death.*
(Proverbs ch. 23 v. 13)

(Previous page) The beginning of the Book of Proverbs, from the 42-line Bible, printed in Mainz, Germany, about 1453—5. The illuminated capital letter P has a picture of King Solomon in it, who was thought to have written all these wise sayings.

There is still a proverb like this today. Fill in the missing words: 'Spare the _____ and spoil the _____.'
3 *Pride comes before disaster, and arrogance before a fall.*
(Proverbs ch. 16 v. 18)
How is this proverb shortened today?
4 Read Proverbs ch. 11 vv. 16—25.
   a) Copy out the most colourful saying.
   b) Copy out one proverb which is outrightly religious.
   c) Copy out one proverb which you think is common sense and teaches how to get on in life.
   d) Copy out one proverb which has a moral lesson i.e. it teaches what is right and wrong.
5 Psalm 49 is a Wisdom song, as you will see by reading vv. 1—4. The rest of the psalm is on a common Wisdom theme: that life is short, so we should make the most of it while we can. Find the verses which are most like today's sayings: 'You're a long time dead' and 'You can't take it with you.'
6 a) Look up the *History Chart* on page 7 to find out when King Solomon lived.
   b) Read the famous story of Solomon and the Queen of Sheba in I Kings ch. 10 vv. 1—10. This shows us his fame for wisdom.

Job

Most of the Old Testament takes the view that suffering is a punishment from God, which we bring upon ourselves. In early times it was accepted that the whole community would suffer for any sins that were committed within it. During the monarchy, the king represented the whole community so that if he were good, then the whole nation should prosper, and vice versa. By the sixth century this view was changing to the belief that individuals should answer to God for themselves. Even so, the idea continued to exist that goodness brings rewards, and wickedness brings suffering. Most Wisdom writings also assumed this, but the book of

Satan smiting Job with sore boils, painted by William Blake around 1826.

Job was written to challenge this simple answer to the problem of suffering.

Assignments

7 Discuss in class whether you still assume that life is, or ought to be, fair. (Certain popular sayings would suggest that people do still hold this view, e.g. 'What have I done to deserve this?' and 'Be sure your sins will find you out.')

8 It was only in late biblical times that people began to look forward to an afterlife. Before this they expected all rewards and punishments to come during this lifetime. How does the idea of heaven and hell make more sense of life and of belief in a just God?

The story of Job is of a religious and upright man who was blessed by God with all that he could wish for in life. Then we are told that in the Heavenly Court, the prosecuting angel (Satan) suggested that Job was only good because he was being rewarded so handsomely, but that he would soon lose his faith if things did not go so well for him. So God allowed Job to be put to the test. One disaster came upon another until Job had lost all his ten children and all his property. But his faith remained firm:

> Naked I came from the womb,
> naked I shall return whence I came.
> The LORD gives and the LORD takes away; blessed be the name of the LORD.
> (Job ch. 1 v. 21)

Then Satan tested him more severely by making him so ill that he was covered in sores from head to foot. At first he accepted even this:

> 'If we accept good from God, shall we not accept evil?' (Job ch. 2 v. 10)

After a week of being in agony like this, Job could stand it no longer and he began to curse the day that he was born. Not only did he complain of his physical suffering but, worst of all, God seemed to have deserted him in his hour of need. Three friends had come to comfort him (a fourth was added to the book later) and when they heard his death-wish, each in turn tried to reason with him. Their arguments all boiled down to the traditional answer to suffering: that God is just and only punishes the wicked. Bad people may appear to get away with it for a time, but their sins will catch up with them. They said that no one is perfect and even Job must have sinned in some way. According to their view, Job should have accepted his punishment and repented of his sins so that God could forgive him and start to put things right again.

Job knew that he had done nothing to deserve such suffering and he refused to accept it in silence:

> But I will not hold my peace;
> I will speak out in the distress of my mind
> and complain in the bitterness of my soul.
> (Job ch. 7 v. 11)

He could see that life was *not* always fair: that the innocent often suffered whilst the wicked prospered. He even blamed God for his suffering. Finally, after Job had gone on and on, God answered him out of a whirlwind. His speech put Job in his place: God was the Creator and Job was only a creature:

> Who is this whose ignorant words
> cloud my design in darkness?
> Brace yourself and stand up like a man;
> *I* will ask questions, and *you* shall answer.
> Where were you when I laid the earth's
> foundations?
> Tell me, if you know and understand.
> (Job ch. 38 vv. 2—4)

Job had to admit that God's Wisdom was beyond man's understanding. In the presence of God's majesty and power, he was finally silenced. He had come to a new understanding of God and a deeper relationship with him:

Then Job answered the Lord:

> I know that thou canst do all things
> and that no purpose is beyond thee.
> But I have spoken of great things which I
> have not understood,
> things too wonderful for me to know.
> I knew of thee then only by report,
> but now I see thee with my own eyes.
> Therefore I melt away;
> I repent in dust and ashes.
> (Job ch. 42 vv. 1—6)

In the course of this book, different views are argued out but the problem of innocent suffering is never properly answered. Yet Job's faith was strengthened and he came to trust in God to know what was best for him. He found that his suffering was easier to bear, now that he realised that God had been listening to him and had *not* deserted him in his suffering.

The story ends with Job being restored to good health and fortune. He had a new family and lived long enough to enjoy them. This happy ending to the story of Job may not be very true to life, but it was a way of showing that God would bring people through their suffering and use it for good, at a time when there was no belief in an active afterlife.

Assignments

9 We still use the term 'a Job's comforter'. It describes a person who comes along to comfort someone, but makes matters worse by what they say. Write an imaginary story of any situation where this might happen today.

10 The book of Job was written by an original thinker who challenged the accepted views of his age. He showed that it can sometimes be good to question accepted beliefs, for only in this way can man's knowledge and understanding grow.

Every cloud has a silver lining.

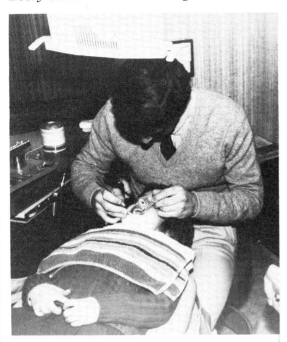

1 Where was this photograph taken?
2 How would you feel if you were the person in the chair?
3 You normally have to make an appointment to see the dentist. What would happen if you had a bad toothache and needed emergency treatment?
4 How has dental treatment improved through the ages?
5 How can a toothache act as a warning system to prevent something much worse happening?
6 What good resolutions might a person make after having dental treatment?

From this one example, it is possible to see that good can sometimes come from suffering. It can alert us to danger. It can bring out compassion in others. It can lead to developments in scientific knowledge. It can make a person more careful about how he treats his body.

a) Can you think of any examples where established beliefs have been challenged? (e.g. Columbus refused to believe that the earth was flat and so discovered other parts of the world.)
b) Write down any religious beliefs you have been taught, which you find difficult to accept.

12 The end

Daniel

The book of Daniel can be found in the Old Testament between the Major and the Minor Prophets, but it does not belong to either of these. Most scholars do not regard it as a prophetic book, but as a type of writing which is called **apocalyptic**. This word comes from Greek and means 'to reveal'. An apocalypse was a revelation of what would happen at the end of the world, usually unfolded in visions.

This type of writing developed at the end of the Old Testament period. It was a kind of escapism when life became too difficult. When the Jews could hardly bear to suffer any more and, humanly speaking, there seemed to be no hope for the future, then they could fix their minds on the thought that God would triumph in the end. Apocalyptic writings encouraged the Jews to hold on to their beliefs, no matter what happened. In fact, the worse things got for them, the better it was in a way, for this was taken as a sign that God would act very soon.

One of the marks of this type of writing was that it was in code-language, using all kinds of mysterious symbols. Otherwise there would have been trouble if it had fallen into the hands of the enemy. For the same reason, the author of the book does not tell us his real name. He takes the name of a hero from the past, called Daniel, meaning 'God is judge'. So this book was symbolic: it stood for something else and was not to be taken at its face-value. The first half of the book tells of the adventures of Daniel and his three friends; and the last half records four visions that Daniel saw, as if he were describing them.

Assignments

1 In our day, the word **apocalypse** has come to be used for terrible disasters (as in the film *Apocalypse Now*). Disasters are certainly foretold in apocalyptic writings, but what does the word 'apocalypse' actually mean?
2 a) If apocalyptic stories were a kind of escapism, what types of stories might be their equivalent today?
  b) Can you think of any other ways that people escape from reality today, apart from through stories? (Consider how people escape from boredom; how they take their minds off the same daily routine; how they avoid thinking about the possible horrors of this nuclear age etc.)
3 a) In pairs, work out a simple code-language.
  b) Write each other a short message in this code and try to decipher the one you receive.

The story is set in the time of the Exile, when Daniel and his friends were young Jews growing up in Babylon. This too, was a way of keeping secret the real purpose of the book. What may have looked like a story of long ago and far away, and like a fairy-tale with strange beasts and so on, was in fact a revolutionary book and highly dangerous. There are many reasons to believe that it was written a lot later than the Exile, in the second century BC. This was another period when Judaism had a struggle to survive. The Persian empire had given way to the Greek empire, and Greek ideas and ways of life had become well established in Palestine and posed a great threat to Judaism. Many 'modern' Jews, especially the younger generation, were turning their backs on the 'old-fashioned' religion of their fathers and were being swept along with these new ideas.

Things came to a head when King Antiochus IV came to power. He believed that he was the god, Zeus, come down to earth and that it was his job to stamp out other religions, like Judaism, and force people to worship Zeus. He forbade the Jews to follow their religious laws and put to death

A statue of Zeus in Rome. The thunderbolt in his left hand and the eagle symbolise his power. The eagle was also an emblem of the Roman Empire.

many who disobeyed. The Jews could take no more when Antiochus dared to set up a statue of Zeus in the sacred temple of Jerusalem. The following passage, written as if looking into the future, seems to refer to this:

> 'Armed forces dispatched by him will desecrate the sanctuary and the citadel and do away with the regular offering. And there they will set up "the abominable thing that causes desolation".' (Daniel ch. 11 v. 31)

A rebellion flared up which grew into the Maccabean Wars. These stretched on for about twenty-five years but they brought the Jews victory.

Most scholars believe that the book of Daniel was like an 'underground magazine', written in the Maccabean times. It was produced and passed round secretly, to encourage the faithful Jews to fight on. Yet it was written in code so that, even if they found it, their enemies would not realise what it meant. Its hidden message was that God still cared for his chosen people, even when it seemed that wicked, worldly rulers had the upper hand. It reminded its readers that God had always kept the covenant with them and he still loved them. God had not deserted them in the past, even when Jerusalem was destroyed and the Jews had been taken far away into Exile; and he would not desert them now.

The book opens with the story of the four young Jews being brought up to serve at the court of the king of Babylon. They refused to eat the rich food available there, preferring to be vegetarians rather than to eat any meat that was forbidden to Jews. Yet, we are told, they looked healthier and were better nourished than the rest.

Jews have many laws which govern what they can eat and how it should be prepared. These laws became very important after the Exile, under the direction of the priests, and set Jews apart from the Gentiles. Antiochus had forbidden them to observe these laws. This story, therefore, would have encouraged Jews of the second century to defy the king, assuring them that they would be better for it.

Assignments

4 a) Do you know of any Jewish food laws?
  b) Look up Leviticus ch. 11 vv. 4—8 and list the four animals named there that Jews are forbidden to eat.
  c) Read the passage in Leviticus again to find out why these animals were forbidden. Using the same argument, work out if a deer or a horse are permitted or forbidden.
  d) If you want to know more forbidden or permitted (kosher) foods, read the rest of Leviticus ch. 11.
5 a) Does your school make any allowances for people with special food requirements?
  b) If you ate different foods from your friends, how might this set you apart from them?

Daniel's three friends, Shadrach, Meshach and Abed-nego, were favourites with the king until he heard that they refused to bow down to a huge golden statue that he had set up. When they were brought before him, they still insisted that they would only worship God, even under pain of death. The king was furious and had a furnace heated so high that his strongest soldiers were killed by the heat when they threw in the three Jews. When the king looked into the fire, he saw four men walking in it! He thought the fourth must be an angel and, when he called to them, the three young men came out of the furnace completely unharmed. The king was greatly impressed by the God of the Jews.

The readers of this story would not necessarily expect God to protect them from harm, for many of their friends and relatives had already given their lives for their faith. But this story of courage and victory might have encouraged them to stand up for their religion during the difficult years of Antiochus' persecution, in the belief that Judaism would win through in the end.

Another famous story with a similar meaning is Daniel in the Lions' Den. This takes place in the reign of another king and Daniel is thrown to the lions for praying three times a day to God, as was the Jewish custom. Daniel was as good as dead: a stone sealed the mouth of the pit, like a tomb. Yet the next morning when the pit was opened, Daniel was alive and well. The story ends with the king giving his support to Judaism.

Assignments

6 Perhaps your class could learn the Negro spiritual about Shadrach, Meshach and Abed-nego.
7 Take either of the two stories above and write it out as a play in your own words.
8 Look up the poem in Daniel ch. 6 vv. 26—7. Which words, used to describe God, would be most encouraging to the Jews of the second century?
9 The theme of wild animals refusing to harm someone is found in other stories. It symbolises the goodness of the person involved and that he is in the right. Try to find out the story of Saint Francis on this theme.

Now we come to Daniel's visions. In the first, he saw four huge beasts coming up out of the sea; the last had ten horns and was the most dreadful of all. This is how it goes on:

> I kept looking, and then
>   thrones were set in place and one
>   ancient in years took his seat,
>   his robe was white as snow and the hair
>   of his head like cleanest wool.
> Flames of fire were his throne and its
>   wheels blazing fire;
> a flowing river of fire streamed out
>   before him.
> Thousands upon thousands served him
>   and myriads upon myriads attended his
>   presence.
> The court sat, and the books were
>   opened.
> (Daniel ch. 7 vv. 9—10)

90

This painting by Briton Riviere (1840–1920) shows Daniel in the lions' den. Describe the attitude of Daniel and of the lions in this picture.

The last beast was killed and the others brought under control. Daniel was still watching when, he says,

> I saw one like a man coming with the clouds of heaven; he approached the Ancient in Years and was presented to him. Sovereignty and glory and kingly power were given to him, so that all people and nations of every language should serve him . . . (vv. 13–14a)

We are told that the four beasts represent four kingdoms. Most likely they stand for the Assyrian, Babylonian, Persian and Greek empires (with Antiochus as one of the horns), all of which had swallowed up Palestine in their day. Life was almost unbearable for a faithful Jew under the fourth empire, but the interpretation of the vision ends with this promise:

> 'The kingly power, sovereignty, and greatness of all the kingdoms under heaven shall be given to the people of the saints of the Most High. Their kingly power is an everlasting power and all sovereignties shall serve them and obey them.' (v. 27)

Assignments

10 How do you know that the 'Ancient in Years' is God and on the side of goodness? What symbols represent this?
11 Why is the name **Daniel**, meaning 'God is judge', a very suitable title for this book?

The son of man

Daniel spoke of the coming of 'one like a man'. Other translations have 'one like a *son of man*', which later became a title for the Messiah. In the Old Testament the phrase 'son of man' was just another way of saying 'man': like our expression 'every mother's son' for 'everyone'. In the vision, one man approaches the Ancient in Years and is given kingly power over all nations. So it is easy to see why the Messiah was later called the Son of Man. But the interpretation given here makes it quite clear that this man, or 'son of man', in the vision was a symbol to represent all the 'saints of the Most High'. He stood for all the faithful Jews who had suffered for their religion. These Jewish saints would inherit the kingdom of God.

In the last chapter of Daniel we find an idea which only developed towards the end of the Old Testament period: that of resurrection to new life after death, in heaven or hell.

> But at that moment your people will be
>   delivered,
>   every one who is written in the book:
> many of those who sleep in the dust of
>   the earth will wake,
>   some to everlasting life
>   and some to the reproach of eternal
>   abhorrence.
> (Daniel ch. 12 v. 2)

There had been many Jewish martyrs in the second century who had given their lives for their faith. The book of Daniel assures the Jews under persecution that not only will God win the final victory but, at the end of this wicked age, the faithful will be raised to new life and everlasting glory. Come what may, the final score of the match between good and evil was already known. The Jews could endure the suffering and risk their necks because they knew they were on the winning side.

So we see that this, the latest of the Old Testament writings, ends on the victorious note that the People of God will triumph in the end. This, indeed, is the main message of the Old Testament story: that faithfulness to God is rewarded.

Assignment

12 What do you think happens to us after death? Give your reasons.

Index